The Endles

C000281135

Rifleman James Andrew Flanagan, The Royal Rifles of
Canada, Regimental Number E30353 circa 1945. AFC

The Endless Battle

The Fall of Hong Kong and Canadian POWs in Imperial Japan

Andy Flanagan
with a foreword by Franco David Macri

GOOSE LANE EDITIONS AND
THE GREGG CENTRE FOR THE STUDY OF WAR AND SOCIETY

Copyright © 2017 by Andy Flanagan.

All rights reserved. No part of this work may be reproduced or used in any form or by any means, electronic or mechanical, including photocopying, recording, or any retrieval system, without the prior written permission of the publisher or a licence from the Canadian Copyright Licensing Agency (Access Copyright). To contact Access Copyright, visit www.accesscopyright.ca or call 1-800-893-5777.

Edited by J. Brent Wilson.
Cover design by Julie Scriver.
Front Cover: Canadian soldiers parading at Hong Kong before the Japanese attack. LAC PA-34182
Page layout by Jaye Haworth, JayeDesign.com.
Frontispiece: Rifleman James Andrew Flanagan, The Royal Rifles of Canada, Regimental Number E30353 circa 1945. AFC
Printed in Canada.
10 9 8 7 6 5 4 3 2 1

Library and Archives Canada Cataloguing in Publication

Flanagan, Andy, 1955-, author
     The endless battle : the fall of Hong Kong and Canadian POWs in imperial Japan / Andy Flanagan.

(New Brunswick military heritage series ; 24)
Includes bibliographical references and index.
Issued in print and electronic formats.
ISBN 978-1-77310-005-0 (softcover).--ISBN 978-1-77310-006-7 (EPUB).-- ISBN 978-1-77310-007-4 (Kindle)

     1. Hong Kong (China)--History--Siege, 1941. 2. Canada. Canadian Army--History--World War, 1939-1945. 3. World War, 1939-1945--Prisoners and prisons, Japanese. 4. Prisoners of war--Canada--Biography. 5. Prisoners of war--Japan--Biography. 6. World War, 1939-1945--Canada. 7. World War, 1939-1945--Campaigns--China--Hong Kong. I. Title. II. Series: New Brunswick military heritage series ; 24

D767.3.F63 2017   940.54'25125   C2017-902925-8
                                                 C2017-902926-6

We acknowledge the generous support of the Government of Canada, the Canada Council for the Arts, and the Government of New Brunswick.

Goose Lane Editions
500 Beaverbrook Court, Suite 330
Fredericton, New Brunswick
CANADA E3B 5X4
www.gooselane.com

New Brunswick Military History Project
The Brigadier Milton F. Gregg, VC,
Centre for the Study of War and Society
University of New Brunswick
PO Box 4400
Fredericton, New Brunswick
CANADA E3B 5A3
www.unb.ca/nbmhp

RECYCLED
Paper made from recycled material
FSC   FSC® C103567

Dedicated to the men from the Jacquet River, New Brunswick area, who are buried in the Far East. These brave men fought the way a soldier would and died the way a soldier should, brave to the very end:

Robert M. Barclay—at Sham Shui Po POW Camp,
Hong Kong, age 24
Edmund Bertin—at St. Stephen's College Hospital, age 26
James Blair Firlotte—at Yokohama POW Camp, Japan, age 38
John F. Firlotte—in battle, age 23
Gabriel Guitard—at Yokohama POW Camp, Japan, age 31
Charles Gordon Hickey—in battle, age 20
Fidele Legacy—at Sham Shui Po POW Camp,
Hong Kong, age 36
Arthur McAllister—at Sham Shui Po POW Camp,
Hong Kong, age 35
John McKay—at St. Stephen's College Hospital, age 22
Henry William Noel—in battle, age 20
Raymond Splude—at Sham Shui Po POW Camp,
Hong Kong, age 39

Contents

Foreword

After fighting the Chinese to a standstill in the early years of World War II, Japanese leaders tried to break the deadlock they created by launching an offensive across the Pacific in December 1941. A number of factors underpinned this strategy, but one of the most important was the desire to cut external support for China's war effort. Thus, the decision was made in Tokyo to expand the war by attacking British and American forces. Shortly before that, in the fall of 1941, Canada sent two battalions of infantry to Hong Kong. Reinforcement of Hong Kong's garrison was assigned to The Winnipeg Grenadiers and The Royal Rifles of Canada. This responsibility was assumed by the Canadian government, under the leadership of Prime Minister W.L. Mackenzie King, in order that Canada could strengthen Anglo-American coalition-building efforts in China. As the war became truly global in scope, these soldiers soon found themselves caught in the maelstrom that spread across East Asia into the Southwest Pacific. Those who defended Hong Kong and survived the battle faced the remainder of this struggle under the most precarious conditions as prisoners of war (POWs). At the end in August 1945, one in four Canadians sent to Hong Kong would not return home.

Much has been written since that time about the Battle of Hong Kong and its aftermath. Few eyewitness accounts, such as the diary of Captain Harry White (at the Canadian War Museum), survived into the postwar era, as it was difficult for POWs to keep written records safe while in captivity. Consequently, the first documents to appear were often government reports from officials in Ottawa, London, and even Washington. Books and articles were published over the following decades. Some were written as military histories while others focused on intelligence or geopolitical issues, but biographies and personal memoirs constitute essential elements of the historiography that aid our understanding of that time. These works, whether they be published volumes or unpublished manuscripts found in archives, serve the function of reminding readers about the impact of total war on average people, particularly the cost paid by those involved directly.

Andy Flanagan's *The Endless Battle: The Fall of Hong Kong and Canadian POWs in Imperial Japan* is one such valuable and poignant book. Flanagan details the experiences of his father, Rifleman James Andrew "Ando" Flanagan of The Royal Rifles of Canada, both during the war and after. Based largely on his father's letters and notes, this book gives readers a sense of some of the hardships faced by prisoners of the Japanese Empire. Moreover, it also provides a glimpse of some of the popular motivations and impulses encouraging enlistment within Canadian society during the early part of the war. In some ways this work is similar to Sergeant-Major George MacDonell's *A Soldier's Story: From the Fall of Hong Kong to the Defeat of Japan* (2002), or even Laura Hillenbrand's American account of Lieutenant Louis Zamperini's ordeal in *Unbroken: A World War II Story of Survival, Resilience, and Redemption* (2010). *The Endless Battle* is different however, in that it focuses on New Brunswick's Hong Kong volunteers. In much of the existing literature, The Royal Rifles of Canada is described largely as a Quebec-based regiment. Occasionally, one may find a brief statement or footnote indicating that others were included in its ranks, but *The Endless Battle* devotes close attention to those who joined from the Jacquet River area. Because of this, we can see that the Battle of Hong Kong had a wider impact than was previously understood. Ultimately, *The Endless Battle* helps fill a historical gap in Canada's military history that has long been neglected, and serves as a useful addition to the historiography on the Battle of Hong Kong.

FRANCO DAVID MACRI

Introduction

At age twenty-five, James Andrew Flanagan began an adventure he believed might add a little excitement to his life. He enlisted in The Royal Rifles of Canada and soon found himself on a ship heading to war in the Far East, accompanied by thirty-seven friends from his hometown area of Jacquet River, New Brunswick. This was the first group of Canadian soldiers to see battle in the Second World War. As Flanagan and his fellow young comrades encountered the cruel depths of war, his exciting journey quickly turned into a never-ending nightmare.

Within what is arguably the last untold story of the Second World War, we are introduced to the realities of war and the extreme hardship these soldiers endured. This is a story every Canadian deserves to hear. Using original source documents we follow Andrew Flanagan's unforgettable journey. It is both tear wrenching and, at times, comical as we see these young soldiers endure terrible experiences and try to add a little humour to their otherwise dismal lives.

Through this account we meet several young New Brunswick men who faced the pain of war together as they courageously fought to defend Hong Kong. Though they were outnumbered by the Japanese Imperial Army and had few or no reinforcements, giving up was out of the question for this group of courageous fighters; they were prepared to fight till their death to defend the island. Nevertheless, on Christmas Day 1941, Hong Kong's defenders were ordered to surrender to the Japanese. Flanagan and his surviving Canadian comrades were forced to endure three and a half years of unforgettable hardship as prisoners of war (POWs). Flanagan watched his comrades and friends die from hunger and disease, while he, also hurting, slowly declined. He was forced to work long, hard days with little or no food, and was subjected to persistent inhumane beatings that would haunt him for the rest of his life.

On August 15, 1945, the Japanese surrendered, Andrew's war ended, and the survivors of the Royal Rifles were finally freed. As readers, we take part in the celebrations, as these brave soldiers were welcomed back to Canada. We watch as Flanagan was reunited with his crying mother who was unsure, for the longest time, whether Andrew was dead or alive. Only twenty-seven local veterans got off the train that day. The other eleven men remained at stand-to in Asia forever. They were dead but not forgotten, according to Andrew.

Flanagan resumed his civilian life after losing four years to the war. He married and started a family of his own. But the love of his family could not keep the nightmares away. The images of war haunted his soul. Sometimes in his uneasy rest he screamed in Japanese as he revisited the horrors of his endless battle.

James Andrew Flanagan finally joined his fallen comrades on February 27, 1993. His story continued to be told through the recorded reminiscences and diary entries he left behind. Throughout this book these sources give the old soldier a voice and a place in Canadian history.

Dr. S.P. Smith, an Oxford scholar and Andrew Flanagan's long-time employer, once told him that history belonged to the victorious. But Andrew's story is not about winning or the victorious. He simply survived.

By today's standards, this manuscript is not politically correct. Commonplace terms, idioms, and language of the time are used to describe the enemy and the events of Andrew's war. His story is narrated the way he lived it as a Canadian soldier in the Far East during the Second World War. With his storytelling, Andrew made it clear that he did not harbour hatred for Japanese people. He would say that during the war the average civilians in Japan were almost as desperate as he was. However, he was adamant about his disdain for the cruel individual guards who beat him and caused his comrades to suffer and die. He said many times that he loathed the Japanese authorities of that time for developing such a horrific war machine, which unleashed unthinkable misery and destruction on the world and the Japanese people.

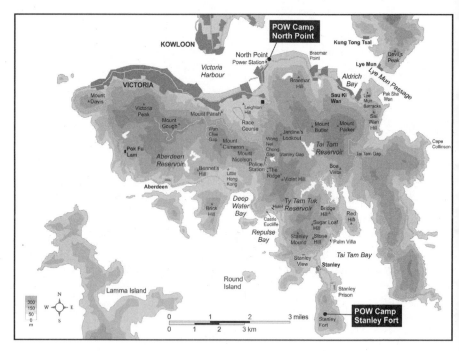

Map of the Battle of Hong Kong. MB

Chapter One

Setting the Scene

The story of Andrew Flanagan's wartime experiences has its origins in the Far East many years before the Japanese attacked Hong Kong in December 1941. During the First World War Japan allied itself with other nations, including the United Kingdom and members of the British Empire, by declaring war on Germany in 1914. After the First World War Japan was generally a peaceful nation. However, over the next decade imperialist desires grew as the Japanese sought to expand their control over the Far East. In 1920, Japan joined the League of Nations and became one of its four permanent members. In 1929, Japan signed the Geneva Convention on the ethical treatment of POWs but failed to ratify the rules. During the Second World War Japan would indicate that it would follow the convention, but evidence from POWs at the time would prove that the Japanese did not treat prisoners ethically or follow the Geneva Convention rules.

When Japan conquered Manchuria in 1931 troubles began with the league. On March 27, 1933, Japan withdrew from the league and continued its aggression against China and Russia. Between 1929 and 1939 Russia had to defend itself against many skirmishes led by the Japanese. On July 7, 1937, Japan invaded China, initiating the war in the Pacific.

According to an article by Terry Copp in the journal *Canadian Military History*, "by October 1938 Japan had conquered the area adjacent to Hong Kong and by December 1941 the Japanese 23rd Army in South China deployed four divisions with substantial artillery as well as air and naval units." The massive Japanese war machine was poised to take over most of the Far East, including Hong Kong.

Meanwhile, Germany invaded Poland, unleashing the war in Europe. On June 10, 1940, Germany, Japan, and Italy signed the Tripartite Pact. Together, these nations formed the Axis alliance, the formal name of the aggressors that the Allied powers had to defeat. On December 7, 1941, shortly after the Japanese attacked Pearl Harbor and Hong Kong, Canada, the United States, and Great Britain declared war on the Empire of Japan.

In 1941, Prime Minister William Lyon Mackenzie King committed Canadian troops to the defence of Hong Kong. In "Cocked Hats and Swords and Small, Little Garrisons: Britain, Canada and the Fall of Hong Kong, 1941," author Kent Fedorowich wrote, "Designated 'C' Force and commanded by a veteran of the Great War, Brigadier J.K. Lawson, the Canadian contingent consisting of 1,975 service personnel, was composed of The Royal Rifles of Canada and The Winnipeg Grenadiers and two army nurses, Kathleen G. Christie and Anne May Waters." In Hong Kong the two Canadian battalions were placed under British Major-General C.M. Maltby's overall command. Among the Canadians, New Brunswick was well-represented with two hundred soldiers coming from the province (see Appendix).

Many people asked why King would send inexperienced Canadian soldiers to defend the British colony, and numerous historians have since examined his decision-making process. Historian Franco David Macri, author of *Clash of Empires in South China*, sees a wider, more specific reason that Canada sent troops to Hong Kong. The following is Macri's summary.

> During the Second Sino-Japanese War [which began on July 7, 1937] Hong Kong was a Chinese city of great significance as it became the focal point of imperial conflict in Asia. Hong Kong's strategic military value rested in its port facilities, as these were connected by rail to China's Ninth War Zone in Hunan. Throughout the course of the war, Hong Kong served as the most significant conduit of military supplies sustaining Chinese resistance.
>
> Because of this situation Hong Kong became a city of geopolitical importance; it was the nexus of coalition

building efforts by several large powers. Soviet advisers helped sustain the Chinese army, particularly in southern China. Later, American intervention in China rose steadily throughout 1941. This led to the reinforcement of Hong Kong with forces from America's Canadian ally to indicate that additional support would follow. Throughout this period the British maintained open logistical doors at Hong Kong and Rangoon. Although the formation of an anti-fascist front did not succeed initially, the rising level of US intervention meant that the Japanese window of opportunity was closing. Thus, the Japanese attacked Pearl Harbor and began a fateful campaign in the Southwest Pacific during December 1941. Part of the opening act included battles at Hong Kong and Changsha to force an end of the war in China. This effort failed in Hunan, and although the Japanese empire expanded rapidly across the Pacific, the result was a Pyrrhic victory at best. British power in Asia was smashed, but for the Japanese, a similar fate was only a matter of time. Hong Kong was an important catalyst that contributed to this process.

However, this book focuses on the personal level of the battle and the subsequent internment of the Canadian soldiers. It does not analyze the broader military aspects of the war. Some of the many assumptions about and reasons for the Canadian deployment in Hong Kong are mentioned in the book only in passing to put the story in a wider context.

Shortly after Japanese forces attacked the US Pacific Fleet at Pearl Harbor, they attacked Hong Kong. On December 8, 1941, at 0600 hours local time they launched an intense attack on the British Crown colony. Focused at first on mainland Hong Kong, the Japanese pushed hard to break through the northern Hong Kong border along the Gin Drinkers Line, the main British forward position.

The Royal Rifles of Canada and The Winnipeg Grenadiers were mostly part of the defences of the island of Hong Kong. Some of The Winnipeg Grenadiers were deployed to Kowloon as the garrison reserve in order to counterattack the Japanese after they broke through the Gin Drinkers Line at Shing Mun Redoubt. After General Maltby gave orders to withdraw from the mainland, the Grenadiers then acted as a covering force to enable the Royal Scots and the Punjab (Indian) troops to pull back.

Air raids and artillery attacks forced the Allied troops to withdraw and move to their defensive positions on the island of Hong Kong. On December 18, following intensive bombing, the Japanese invaded the island. The Japanese attackers were reinforced from the mainland and had total air domination. The defenders' closest reinforcements were thousands of miles away and they had no air defence. The Canadians' heavy equipment landed in the Philippines en route to Hong Kong but had not yet reached the colony. The Canadians had no tanks, only their rifles, a few Bren guns, and trucks, but they fought on. The attackers quickly separated the regiments, dividing the Canadian contingent into two. In spite of the soldiers' valiant efforts, on Christmas Day Hong Kong was forced to surrender. During the afternoon General Maltby advised Governor Mark A. Young that Hong Kong could no longer be defended and the surrender order was issued. The defence of Hong Kong was over. It had taken the Japanese eighteen days to force the surrender. Outnumbered and out-gunned, the brave and ferocious Allied defenders, including the Canadian troops, must be given credit for maintaining the defence for as long as they did. At the end of the battle, 290 Canadians had been killed and an additional 493 wounded. Unofficially, the Japanese had five times more casualties.

The Canadians and other Allied soldiers who survived had to withstand three and a half years of hardship as prisoners of war. Many Canadians died as POWs. Even before the battle had ended, the Canadians suffered cruelty at the hands of the Japanese. On the last day of fighting, the Japanese captured St. Stephen's College, which was being used as a temporary hospital. They raped, assaulted, and murdered nurses, and stabbed wounded Canadian soldiers to death in their beds. The Canadian POWs were imprisoned in Hong Kong and Japan where they suffered brutal treatment, starvation, forced labour, and humiliation. In northern Japan, they slaved for twelve hours a day in mines or on the docks in the cold.

Soldiers from the Royal Rifles at Hong Kong. At centre is John Killoran
from Belledune, NB. IWM LF193

Many of them died. In all, more than 550 of the 1,975 Canadians who fought in the Battle of Hong Kong never returned home. Roughly one third of the 200 New Brunswick soldiers died as a result of their participation in the defence of Hong Kong.

In November 1941, Rifleman James Andrew Flanagan of the Royal Rifles was one of 1,975 Canadian soldiers sent to guard the British colony of Hong Kong. It was no secret that the Japanese imperialist ambition virtually guaranteed an attack on the territory. He didn't know then that the Allies had faint hope of stopping the impending onslaught of Japanese infantry. The British Command hoped the Canadians would bolster the otherwise under-manned Allied defences in Hong Kong. They hoped to hold the Japanese back long enough for many of their loyal subjects stationed in Hong Kong to evacuate. Unfortunately, Andrew didn't know that the Allies' purpose was only to slow the enemy's advance.

He kept a detailed account of the Battle of Hong Kong as well as journal entries for each of the 1,278 days he survived as a POW. After the war, he never missed an opportunity to tell the details of his horrific experience. He wanted the world to know how he and his comrades suffered. He wanted everyone to know the real cost of war. Mostly, he wanted the world to know that sometimes we have to fight for our country for freedom's sake. As he would say, "Don't be fooled; don't let anyone romance war." Andrew, like most combat soldiers, quickly realized that war was not a great adventure. It was a misery that his generation had to endure.

Andrew kept his two-page account of the eighteen-day Battle of Hong Kong hidden in his boot lining throughout his internment. He didn't want the Japanese to censor or confiscate its details like they did periodically with his journals. From time to time the Japanese guards gathered all POW journals and blacked out any reference to the inhuman treatment they suffered, including starving, beatings, and torture. This book is also based on recordings of Andrew recounting the events, transcribed by me, his son. It is an honest attempt to look at the horrors of war and its lingering effects.

In the fall of 1941, when a group of soldiers from the Jacquet River, New Brunswick, area headed off to the Pacific war, the village numbered only a few hundred residents. Eleven of Andrew's friends died in the Far East: three in the actual Battle of Hong Kong (one hacked to death in a hospital for wounded soldiers), the others perished in POW camps.

Listed below are the names of the Jacquet River area soldiers, many of them Andrew's pals, who fought in the Battle of Hong Kong:

Bob Barclay*
John Baskin
Edmund Bertin*
Luke Bujold
Arnold Courier (Carrier)
Norman Cormier
Lyle Dempsey
Abe Driscoll
Bunny Duplassie
Fred Elsliger
Blair Firlotte*
John Firlotte*
Leslie Firlotte
Joe Frenette
Phil Gallie
Wesley Gallon
Gabe Guitard*
Wardie Hamilton
Gordon Hickey*
Paul Hickey

Bill Hickie
John Killoran
Joe Landry
Eugene Lapointe
Fidele Legacy*
Arthur McAllister*
Tom McCarron
John McKay*
Ernie Meade
Ernie Miller
Albert Murchie
Henry Noel*
Leo (Pete) Pitre
Bert Roy
Raymond Splude*
George Steeves
Wendell Thompson

and James Andrew Flanagan

*Died in battle or as a POW

Andrew, age 14, with his grandfather and
namesake Andrew Donnelly. AFC

Chapter Two

Before the War

James Andrew Flanagan was born on February 1, 1914, in the tiny community of St. Margarets, near present-day Miramichi, New Brunswick. He was named after his grandfather Andrew Donnelly. At home the family called him Ando, as a result of his own attempt to pronounce his name at age two. He was the second-oldest child in a family of seven children and he learned at a young age to share the meagre possessions his family owned. His mother, Mary Emma W. Donnelly Flanagan, was a schoolteacher when she had a teaching contract. His father, James William Flanagan, was a subsistence farmer and a cook when he got work with railway labour gangs. His family's house, a cabin along present-day Highway 11 in St. Margarets, provided minimum shelter and little in the way of creature comforts. The shack faced St. Patrick's Church where Andrew developed a fondness for singing in the choir. His family was very poor, but, for the most part, he admitted that he was unaware of or unconcerned with their situation.

Misadventure seemed the norm when Andrew was younger. The events he recounted to his family are testimony to his zest for life and sometimes his recklessness, but also his will to survive. According to his mother, Andrew was always a "talker" who loved to tell stories. In Ireland, she believed, he would have been a bard. His gift for storytelling is evident throughout this book. Andrew always spoke warmheartedly of his youth. Even his misadventures, like his bear tale, one of his many stories that became etched in the memories of his children, had a nostalgic tone of missing the good old days.

One day, as the story goes, Andrew and his older brother Leo were deep in the woods hauling firewood home. The old wagon moaned over every rise and rut on the long trail through the thick brush. Suddenly, as they rounded a bend in the road, a huge black bear stood up on his haunches less than fifteen metres ahead of them. The boys scurried to the top of the load and yelled at the old mare to run. In the excitement the reins dropped to the ground and the old horse instinctively stopped. (The mare, which was deaf and had limited eyesight, took every opportunity to rest.) Leo convinced Andrew to jump to the ground to fetch the reins. In a fit of bravery, he recounted, he leapt down, and as he hit the turf he saw the bear drop to all fours. "I am certain I felt the ground shake as he charged toward me," Andrew would say. He quickly bolted to safety with Leo on top of the wood piled on the wagon. Leo grabbed the reins and slapped the horse's rump as hard as he could. "*GETEEUP!*" Leo yelled at the top of his lungs. The old girl was oblivious to the danger. She turned her head in a defiant manner and as she heaved ever so slowly the wagon crept ahead. When the bear reached the steed something kicked in. The horse reared as high as she could without snapping the shafts that attached her to the wagon. She sprung ahead like a young colt, jolting half the load of wood off. Leo and Andrew fell as the wood rolled from under them but they managed to hang on. In a flash the bear was gone. The horse didn't stop galloping until they reached the barn, where she tried to enter the small man door, wagon and all. The boys' father, who had been watching from the kitchen window, blamed that day for the horse's death later in that same year. Andrew would chuckle, and so ended the story.

One of Andrew's favourite stories from his youth took place after his family moved to the Jacquet River area. He told us how bravery combined with some foolishness saved his dog. By 1921, Andrew's family had outgrown their abode and his parents were fed up with the lack of opportunity in the Miramichi region. They moved to his mother's hometown of Jacquet River, New Brunswick, where they lived for a time with his grandfather, Andrew Donnelly, and grandmother, Maggie (Doyle) Donnelly. Andrew's mother taught for many years afterward at local schools.

By the fall of the first year, Andrew and his family had moved into McRae's house at Belledune River. It was a big, cold house with plenty of room for the whole crowd. One day Andrew's father arrived home with a puppy. It was a mixed breed, predominantly black lab. Andrew and his siblings argued for days about a name for the dog. Finally, his father (Pop) put an end to the scuffle by naming it Pup. The name stuck and every dog the family owned afterward was named Pup.

One Sunday morning in the spring of 1922 Andrew, with his brothers Leo and Roger (Roge), were walking the three miles to their local church. Their dog, Pup, was following them so the boys tried to chase him home. As they were crossing the Belledune River Bridge, Pup disappeared. They assumed he went home and continued to walk to church. On the way home, an hour and a half later, they stopped at the one-lane bridge to watch the melting ice in the river. To their horror Pup was frantically swimming in circles in a small opening in the ice, desperately trying to get out of the raging water. The dog couldn't get a toe hold; every time he tried to scramble out of the hole he fell back, sinking under water for a few seconds. "He'll drown if we don't get him out!" Leo shouted.

Leo warned his younger brothers not to go on the river ice. He told them to wait on the bridge while he ran to the barn to get a rope. By the time Leo returned to the bridge several other local boys and their dogs had gathered. They were all encouraging Pup to crawl out, but by then he was too weak. "He didn't have enough strength to try," Andrew said. Leo decided they had to lower someone down to save Pup.

Andrew was the smallest boy, lightweight, and most times too young or too foolish, as he would say, to be afraid. He was nominated as the one to be lowered. Leo and the other boys tied one end of the rope to Andrew's feet and edged him over the side of the bridge, head first. The younger boys walked down to the bottom of the river bank with their dogs in tow to get a better view of the heroic rescue.

The bridge was eight metres above the water and ice. The rope was eight metres long, with most of one lost due to the knot. As the boys lowered Andrew, they came to the end of the rope. Upside-down Andrew still couldn't quite reach the dog. The boys stretched and leaned over the side of the bridge until he could reach the dog. He seized Pup by his collar with his right hand and yelled for the boys to pull them up. However, the rope either slipped or broke. "The water was dreadfully cold as I plunged in," Andrew would say. He and Pup sank deep into the river where the swift current pulled them under the ice. With his feet tied, he couldn't swim; all he could do was hold onto Pup by the collar. Under the water, he recalled, he heard the other dogs' muffled barks and the frantic screams of the boys. He was sure he was going to die and he felt panicked. His lungs were ready to burst and he envisioned his body in a cold, dark, watery grave. Pup pulled him upward but the ice still entombed them. He tried pounding on the ice but it was too thick to break. Miraculously, he felt a tug on the rope.

When Leo and the other boys stretched over the bridge to give Andrew the extra length he needed to nab Pup, Leo had unwound the rope from his hand. As Andrew seized Pup, the extra weight had caused the rope to pull through Leo's mitted hand. The rope had fallen and landed near the younger boys below the bridge. Leo yelled for the boys to catch the rope and hold on to it until he got there. Leo bounded over the side of the bridge and landed near the younger boys where he grabbed the rope and pulled until Andrew and the dog appeared from the icy abyss.

During his rescue, Andrew said, he was paralyzed with cold, but he held Pup tightly until they were both safely on solid ice. The other boys ran to help. He was shaking uncontrollably and couldn't catch his breath. Leo rolled him on his stomach and water drained from his lungs. He was finally able to inhale between bouts of coughing and puking. The boys put Andrew on a sleigh and wrapped him in their coats. They hauled him home as fast as they could where his mother nervously dressed him in dry clothes, wrapped him in blankets, and laid him on a cot she pulled next to the wood stove. She scolded the other boys and didn't want to hear about Pup. Pop took the dog to the barn to dry off. Although Andrew caught double pneumonia and was sick for a couple of months, he told his brothers (out of his mom's earshot) that it was worth it. "I would do it all over again, if I had to," he concluded. This was the first of many actions that unwittingly shaped the course of Andrew's life.

Andrew stayed in school until he reached Grade 10, the highest grade offered in his community. Then he worked on his father's farm until he got a job as a "Boy Friday" with Dr. Stephen Percy Smith, who had built a retirement cottage at the beach near Andrew's home. Dr. Smith was exceptionally well-educated. At Oxford University, where he was Mansell Exhibitioner of St. John's College, he had earned a doctorate degree in literature. He also earned a diploma in agriculture from Cambridge and studied geology at the University of New Brunswick. Smith was also an experienced architect and apprenticed with his father, Edward Smith, who was a prominent architect in Leeds, England. Andrew worked for the good doctor as a cook, butler, chauffeur, and handyman.

Dr. Smith decided that Andrew did not have an adequate education. His mission to educate the boy included a few hours each day studying English and English grammar, Latin, Greek, and any other subject where Andrew demonstrated weaknesses. Dr. Smith was a good man, according to Andrew. He said that Smith invoked a lifelong love for learning in him.

Dr. Smith, who had fought during the First World War, had expectations that every young, able-bodied man should do the same in the Second World War. Andrew told him that he wanted to enlist, but he also explained his reluctance to leave Smith without an assistant. Upon hearing this, Andrew said, Smith raised his voice, exclaiming, "Ando, it is our duty to defend what we believe in. If you join the war effort, I will do my share by not wasting a young potential fighting man on my servitude. I will also keep your position until you return." Dr. Smith remained true to his word. On occasion local men would ask for Andrew's job while he was away at war, but Smith belittled them in a way that only an Oxford man could. Andrew's father overheard him tell a young lad that he should be fighting for his country, not trying to poach Andrew's job. As the young man left, Dr. Smith reportedly said to Andrew's father, "I have never witnessed such an exhibition of ignorance in all my life."

Another of Andrew's prewar stories took place just before he joined the army. He was engaged in what most young men of his age were doing…trying to impress the girls. That summer he and his brother Leo spent much of their free time at the beach in Jacquet River, diving from the rocks. He said he had his eye on two local girls. One day, near the end of July 1940, one of the girls, named Violette, dared him to dive into the water, but Andrew hesitated. During part of the summer the Bay of Chaleur has an unusually high number of jellyfish. To avoid them, it is safest to swim when the tide is receding. Violette taunted him: "You want to join the army, but you're afraid of a few jellyfish." Fully understanding the risk, he protested, saying, "The tide is coming in." She retorted, "So, when the Nazis shoot at you, whatcha gonna do…wait till they run out of bullets?" Penelope, the other girl, shouted for Andrew to ignore Violette. Too late, he accepted the challenge. He climbed to the highest point on Turvey's Rock. The water was murky, but, not seeing any jellyfish, he sprang out and dove like a rock, cutting the water perfectly, without a splash. He said he touched the sandy bottom three or four metres down then spun around and made for the surface. As he emerged he realized he had surfaced in the middle of a huge jellyfish. On shore he quickly tore the hot stinging material from every part of his body. It burned like hell. "I'm on fire!" he shouted.

"Uric acid is the only thing that helps the pain," Leo called.

"What's that? Where do I get it?" Andrew asked.

"It's in piss." Leo laughed.

Before everyone, Andrew urinated all over himself. It worked for the pain but did little for his reputation with the girls. Andrew would end this story by saying, "On the bright side, I didn't leave a girl behind when I joined the army."

Chapter Three

Joining the Army

In July 1940, a recruitment poster at the local hotel in Jacquet River caught Andrew's attention. The Royal Rifles of Canada (RRC), a militia regiment headquartered in Quebec City, had been mobilized and was looking for soldiers. With Fidele Legacy, Fred Elsliger, and a few other friends, Andrew drove to Matapédia, Quebec, to enlist in the army. After the paperwork was completed the recruiting officer sent the men for a medical. The doctor told Andrew that he could not join because he weighed only 112 pounds; he had to weigh at least 115 pounds to join. Andrew told this story with as much pride as possible. He said he walked over to the nearest hotel where he met the other boys and drank six beers in an hour without urinating. "I went back to be reweighed — and I was accepted," Andrew would say smugly. "The doctor shook his head when I told him what I had done. I think he was trying to give me a chance to stay out of the army, but I was determined to fight."

On the drive home the friends talked about how they would spend their pay. During the Dirty Thirties most of the fellows around their hometown didn't have money. Andrew was one of the lucky ones, having a permanent job working for Dr. Smith during the Depression.

Shortly after signing up, Andrew received a letter instructing him to report to The Royal Rifles of Canada at Valcartier, Quebec. Boot camp was what he called it. Thirty-eight men from Andrew's area were accepted into the regiment. All of them boarded the Ocean Limited train at 2000 hours in Jacquet River heading to Valcartier. They joined a few other men from Moncton and Bathurst. The Royal Rifles recruits had half the train

Recruiting poster for The Royal Rifles of Canada. CWM 1970036-024.

to themselves. Many more boarded the train at stops in Campbellton and throughout Quebec.

Some of the boys had booze, Andrew recalled. "We sang songs and told stories late into the night. Like most of the fellows, I was very excited to be leaving Jacquet River. This was my first train trip and my first time being away from home. I couldn't help but wonder what great adventures and places the war would bring." He met Ron Kinnie from Beaver Brook in Albert County that night. Ron would become one of Andrew's best friends.

Just before daylight they were hurried off the train and onto a waiting bus at Quebec City. In Valcartier they stopped in front of the mess hall. According to Andrew, a burly sergeant climbed in and shouted that the recruits had twenty minutes to eat breakfast. They regrouped by the bus at 0700 hours.

Army life wasn't all that bad. It had a few more rules than most of the boys were used to, but it was tolerable when they were in Canada, Andrew said. Boot camp was a wakeup call for most of them. Some quit, one got drummed out. The weeks passed quickly and before he knew it the regiment was on its way to Sussex, NB. "Goodbye and good riddance, I'll not miss you, boot camp," Andrew said as he boarded the bus, bound for a new adventure.

At the camp in Sussex the regiment trained for war. Andrew said he made many new friends there and, for the most part, he had a good time. The barracks were new but not quite completed when they first arrived. The windows were not installed, and the toilets had no dividing walls. It wouldn't do to be shy there, Andrew said. "Thank God the windows and other improvements were completed before it got too cold."

Andrew and Ron Kinnie were assigned to HQ (Headquarters) Company. Andrew became batman to Major Malcolm T.G. MacAulay, who commanded the company. Basically, he was a servant to the major. He said that after the war he found out that he got the job because Dr. Smith was the headmaster of Bishop's College School where MacAulay studied. Apparently, Smith had contacted MacAulay and asked him to take Andrew under his wing.

As his batman, Andrew would do just about anything the major requested. Most mornings his first job was to bring in fellows who were on report. He had to go out and find the men who had gotten in trouble the night before and parade them in front of the major, who would dispense swift justice. Andrew told an adventure story where he almost felt the major's justice.

A few of us had finally been granted three days' leave. When five or six of the boys from Jacquet River heard I was planning to drive home, they jumped in my old Ford with me. This was the first time we went home since we joined the army. The drive was swift, fuelled by a few stops at various bootleggers. The three days passed just as swiftly with many more bootlegger stops. Before we knew it, time was up. In fact, we were past curfew before we even left home for Sussex. We approached the barracks gate well past 0200. I didn't stop, knowing well what the major did to curfew breakers. I tramped the accelerator of the old car and crashed the gate. We sped down the road and pulled in behind the nearest barracks.

When I appeared before Major MacAulay the next morning he handed me a blank page and said that if I caught the asshole that ran the gate the night before, I was to drag him in immediately. "Yes Sir!" I responded, sheepishly asking if he knew the culprit. "Flanagan!" the Major bellowed. "Listen to me, you get away with what you can in this man's army, but if you're caught you get the same punishment as the rest."

Andrew realized that the major knew the perpetrator of the gate ramming. "Dismissed!" finalized his not-so-very-discreet warning.

After this near miss with the major, Andrew inspected his car. The back light on the driver side had been shot out. The bullet was lodged in the frame of the back seat. The guards must have shot at the car as they crashed the gate. "Another close call," Andrew would say with a laugh at the end of this story.

A few weeks after Andrew's gate incident the Royal Rifles shipped out to the very small town of Botwood, Newfoundland, where they were charged with guarding the Newfoundland Airport at nearby Gander, which provided fuel to the many flights heading overseas to the European war front and was later home to Royal Canadian Air Force reconnaissance and fighter squadrons. Although Newfoundland was still a British colony, it cooperated closely with Canada, becoming part of the military's Atlantic Command. Members of the Royal Rifles were among the few Canadian troops who served in both the Pacific and Atlantic theatres of operations.

Gander was a small community consisting of an airport, a number of houses, and a few other buildings. When they were not on guard duty the regiment trained for combat using old First World War equipment. The weather was cold, much like home in the winter, Andrew would say, but it seemed to him that Newfoundland got more snow.

On leave the young soldiers of the RRC would take a freight train to Grand Falls where the people treated them well and they had lots of fun, according to Andrew.

> The girls were pretty and the Black Horse beer was something else. The Newfoundlanders had a drink they called Screech. It was powerful strong rum; Jacquet River barley corn was like soda pop in comparison. I only drank it once. The boys told me the next morning that in my drunken state I'd grabbed O'Leary by the ears and wouldn't let him go until he apologized for calling me a herring choker. [Herring choker is a derogatory term used to insult people from New Brunswick.] I avoided O'Leary as much as possible after that night.

The Royal Rifles had an enormous black Newfoundland dog as mascot that was often mistaken for a bear. Well-tempered and obedient, the dog was cherished by the regiment. His first owner lived in Gander where the gentle beast, named Pal, had been dearly loved by the children in the community. In the winter he would often haul them on sleds. One day in his excitement to greet a group of children he'd raised his paw, accidentally scratching a child's face. His owner worried had that he might have to put the dog down, so instead he'd offered the canine to the Royal Rifles as their mascot. The soldiers aptly changed his name to Gander. Gander quickly adapted to military life. He was promoted to sergeant faster than any enlisted man. On parade he proudly marched up front, wearing his sergeant's stripes next to the regimental badge attached to his harness. In fall 1941, Gander accompanied the Royal Rifles to Hong Kong.

In early summer 1941, the regiment was reassigned to St. John's, Newfoundland, for a few weeks. According to Andrew it was a nice change and he liked the city. On the second day after their arrival, a local ladies' club invited the Royal Rifles to a fancy afternoon tea at the Caribou Hut, in the St. John's YMCA. Andrew loved to tell of how they entertained the ladies in St. John's.

It was quite a sight to see these sophisticated ladies attempt to entertain our rowdy group. We, who had just returned from the sticks in Gander, and most of us having come from even smaller places back home, were anything but refined! To even pretend we had any elegance would be false. As the afternoon dragged on, some of the guys begged this Edgar fella from Quebec to get on the stage and provide some entertainment. I didn't know Edgar, but his buddy Phil Doddridge sitting next to me said that Edgar recites "Little Bateese" and "De Stove Pipe Hole" and many other poems. He also says Edgar could tell spicy jokes and loved to be at the centre of attention.

After much cajoling and catcalling, Edgar sauntered onto the stage. He rubbed his bald head with his left hand and pointed to the ladies with his right and said, "You'll have to forgive me for my lack of hair. My head of hair is so thick

Gander, the mascot of The Royal Rifles of Canada. LAC PA-116791

that the army made me get two haircuts, ten minutes apart."
He laughed from the bottom of his gut as he started his rant.

"Me, I don't feel much like telling poems. I'd rather be serious and tell you what life was like when I was younger," he said with a mischievous grin.

He began his story. "My folks were honest, good people, but we were dirt poor. And me, as a young lad I always wanted a bike. I would often ask my father but it did no good. He would say to me, 'You know we have to feed the family before we get a bike.' One morning when I got up my father stopped me and asked, 'Where'd that bike that's outside the house come from?' 'Well,' I told him, 'I was walking down the road last night when this girl stopped her bike and asked if I wanted a ride. I jumped on the bike with her and she drove down the park and into the woods. Well, one thing led to another, and her pants were off. She said to me, 'Edgar, you can take what you want.' The pants were too small, so I took the bike.'" Edgar guffaws at his own joke as we all whoop in laughter. Immediately following the punchline a red-faced lady advised us that the show was over.

Andrew went on to say that they had more fun in those few weeks than at any other time. The last night of their stay in St. John's, Andrew and his buddies ended up at a house where soldiers go to meet women. This was the soldier's "House of the Rising Sun." The house was full of nice girls. When some British sailors arrived, they acted like they owned the place. They made the mistake of arrogantly telling the Jacquet River boys to leave. The fight was on! The Royal Newfoundland Constabulary ended the bout and took a few of the boys off to jail, but Andrew didn't get caught. The next day the regiment shipped out, returning to Valcartier.

Both at St. John's and Valcartier the regiment received much-needed training on new weapons. They also took in strange lectures like how not to get VD and what to do about body crabs. One lad, Andrew said, asked if it was compulsory. Andrew was sure he was asking about the course, not getting VD. The sergeant and most of the others thought he was being a wise guy. "You'll know how compulsory it is to get rid of it, if you ever get VD," the sergeant boomed out over their laughter.

In September, the regiment returned to coast defence duties when they were posted to Saint John, NB. Then, in mid-October 1941, the Royal Rifles were warned for overseas service, whereupon they returned to Valcartier. Andrew said he didn't know where he was going but he could hardly wait to get there. Just before leaving, Andrew asked to have twenty dollars taken out of his pay and sent to his father to make his car payments while he was away. The paymaster told Andrew that he would forward the paperwork.

Chapter Four

The Voyage to Hong Kong

For years after the war, Andrew Flanagan kept a notebook that contained diary entries made by his friend Ron Kinnie from October to December 1941. Thumbing through it, Andrew said, reminded him of how jovial he and his comrades felt before the Battle of Hong Kong. Proud young men, they were, he would say, on their way to a land they knew little about. Adventure eagerly anticipated. "I couldn't imagine the strange sights, sounds, and culture that I would get pulled into. To say I would experience culture shock would be an understatement. I guess I filled my head with noble thoughts of fighting for honour and the romance of war as I fantasized about exciting adventures to come."

Ron's diary documented the voyage across Canada and the Pacific Ocean ending in Hong Kong. A few years before he died, Andrew was videotaped reading Ron's diary. The following is based on both Andrew's memory and Ron's account of the voyage.

On October 23, Andrew and the Royal Rifles departed from Valcartier on a special troop train. They passed through Quebec City, stopped at Montreal, then continued into Ontario where they stopped in Ottawa. They didn't know yet where they were going. They were told upon departure that they would get their orders along the way. On the video, Andrew read an old Montreal newspaper clipping that was stuffed into Ron's diary.

The first battalion of The Royal Rifles of Canada, which is Quebec's own English-speaking unit, was on their first parade through the city since their return from New Brunswick and Newfoundland. Accompanied by

Members of The Royal Rifles of Canada prepare to leave Valcartier for Hong Kong, October 1941. LAC PA-116794

their regimental mascot, a massive black Newfoundland dog, the unit proved to be among the best on parade, showing the value of the intensive training which they had undergone during their stay in both New Brunswick and Newfoundland. The first battalion was under the command of Lt. Col. W.J. Home.

The second day of their journey was uneventful. They continued through Ontario where they stopped at several small towns. The next day the train rolled into Manitoba where it stopped at Winnipeg in the morning and continued on to Saskatoon. In Alberta, they stopped at Edmonton and then moved into the Rockies where the train stopped in Jasper. "I never saw mountains so high or so majestic. I was impressed by Mount Robson, the highest peak in the Canadian Rockies. We then entered British Columbia. I couldn't believe how big our county was. I remembered thinking that we wouldn't stop until we hit the Pacific Ocean. We would no doubt be fighting in the Pacific but I didn't know either place or time."

The long train ride got boring, according to Andrew. They continued through British Columbia to Vancouver, where they disembarked only to immediately board a troopship named HMT *Awatea* at 0900 hours. They remained docked until the evening, when they sailed out into the coastal waters and the ship anchored for the night. At 1000 hours the next day they sailed out into the Pacific Ocean where they rendezvoused with a convoy heading west.

The first night at sea the water was a little rough. Growing up on the shores of the Bay of Chaleur, Andrew was no stranger to boating and never got seasick, but some of the city boys onboard that night had weaker stomachs.

We were sleeping in hammocks, three tiers high. I was on top with big O'Leary on the bottom. Joe Frenette was in the middle. We could hear some of the boys moaning, including O'Leary. He made the mistake of saying that Joe and I, as herring chokers, would probably be the first to get sick. I took a full mouth full of water and handed my canteen to Joe. He did the same. I leaned over as far as I could and blew the water out of my mouth down on O'Leary as I made horrible vomiting noises. Joe did the same as I. Within thirty seconds O'Leary was puking for real. We were splitting our sides laughing at him.

The next day the weather was fine and Andrew spent his free time exploring the ship and avoiding O'Leary. The convoy continued on its westerly course further out into the Pacific. On the third day the weather was nicer yet. The boys were getting over their seasickness and most soldiers spent their time looking over different parts of the ship.

Royal Rifles soldiers and Gander, their mascot, en route to Hong Kong, November 1941. LAC PA-166999

The next day was much hotter. Andrew attended a military funeral for someone he didn't know, but he said he found the service very interesting since he had never seen a burial at sea before. The men practised air raid drills, including lowering of lifeboats, so they would know what to do in the event of an attack.

The hot weather continued, reaching 100° F below deck. The men spent most of their time on the boat deck. Looking over the rail Andrew spotted weird-looking birds flying low and diving every few metres. As he got closer, he realized that they were flying fish. He also saw dolphins and whales. He and many others slept outside on the deck that night. The ship was blacked out and the crew patrolled from 0200 until 0700 hours. A few days later they sighted land at about 0830 hours.

> The ship sailed into Hawaii at quarter past ten, and anchored, where we took on some supplies and fresh water. Several Hawaiian girls danced and sang on the waterfront. I took their picture through the porthole. Hawaii was a very nice place. I mailed some letters and pictures home from there. We didn't get much chance to enjoy paradise. We couldn't get shore leave. The ship sailed out again just after supper that evening.

Photo of Hawaiian dancers on the waterfront taken
by Andrew through ship's porthole. AFC

The next morning Andrew and his comrades learned about their final destination. "Parade was called and our orders were read. We would be sailing on to Hong Kong, China, to perform garrison duty. I knew then and there that we would be fighting the Japanese in the very near future. Hong Kong of all places! I conjured up images of Marco Polo's ancient spice routes and trading exotic goods with Kublai Khan. I read a book about Polo's excursions titled *Marvels of the World*. I couldn't wait to get there."

The novelty of the big ship wore off as they settled into life on board. "Our diaries all sounded the same," Andrew said, "with entries like weather fine today, sea rolling very badly, cleaned rifle, boat drill, and so on." During the day it was once again very hot and most work was suspended until the evening. He heard some of the sailors on board saying the ship was entering a dangerous area just before the international dateline. When they passed the international dateline Andrew said he felt cheated. "I lost a day, but I wasn't an inch closer to Hong Kong," he laughed.

The following day brought a break from the routine when they met and communicated with an American submarine on patrol. They also had physical training on deck because the weather was cooler. Then, the next few days were so hot and sticky that Andrew and the rest of the men did nothing. He said he felt sick from the heat and may have had a touch of sunstroke. The heat wave continued for another two days. Finally the temperature cooled and he felt better. However, he knew they had entered Japanese-controlled waters and the war news stated that talks between the United States and Japan were going very badly. The ship had entered the monsoon climate area, but the sea was calm just before they sighted land. A mile or two offshore the ship dropped anchor. That evening, there was an amateur hour that was broadcast all over the ship and deck lights were on. "We were lit up like a Christmas tree and made plenty of noise. I suspected the brass was letting the locals know that they were not alone, implying that we would protect them. The island people could clearly see us, but some boys didn't think it was Hong Kong. I hoped it was because I was getting pretty antsy. I couldn't wait for the big adventure to begin."

In the morning the ship sailed away, confirming that they were not in Hong Kong. They saw many islands, small and large. That day they docked on the American-controlled island of Luzon at Manila. After seven hours of taking on fresh water and new supplies they sailed away again. Andrew counted twenty-three American submarines and three torpedo boats as they left the harbour. Members of HQ Company, where Andrew was assigned, were issued rifles that day and they were permitted to get their knapsacks from the stowage area.

Canadian troops disembarking on November 16, 1941, from HMCS *Prince Robert* at Kowloon.
LAC PA-037419

Finally, at 0700 hours on November 16, the *Awatea* docked at Kowloon on the mainland across from Hong Kong Island. At about 0800 hours Andrew disembarked with the advance party and boarded a bus for Sham Shui Po barracks on the northern edge of Kowloon. They were to ready the facilities for the other men. "Hong Kong at last! I was so glad to step on land I could have kissed the ground, but it was much too dirty and the whole area stunk like a combination of oil, shit, fish and sweat," Andrew said.

Andrew missed the seven-mile march through Kowloon from the docks to the barracks where the other Canadian soldiers were greeted like heroes. In his book *"C" Force to Hong Kong*, Brereton Greenhous describes the scene by quoting Canadian soldier Ken Combon: "Our two battalions marched down Nathan Road steel helmeted and obviously invincible. The main street of Kowloon was lined by cheering crowds waving small Union Jacks." On their way to the barracks they looked at equipment belonging to the British Middlesex Regiment. They were not impressed; it was old and looked mostly like First World War remnants.

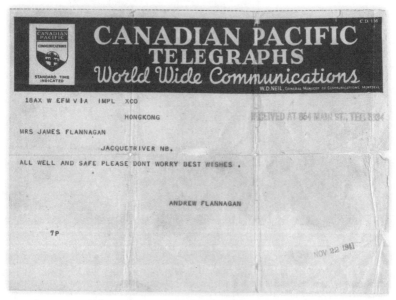

Telegram sent by Andrew notifying his mother
of his arrival in Hong Kong. AFC

Andrew always talked about how different life was over there. The first night they had to sleep with mosquito nets over their beds to protect themselves from mosquitoes and flies to avoid malaria. For the first few days, they collected equipment and performed light duty. They would start work at 0700 but had to quit by noon because of the heat. The evenings were better. Most nights the men were permitted to go into town. During his first night in town, Andrew said, he had a drive in a rickshaw.

Our money was worth a fortune there. We hired our own batmen to shine our boots. At first Hong Kong offered a great life for us. It was hot most of the time, but the nighttime temperatures were like home in the summer. We went out most nights to clubs and restaurants. I saw the strangest things in Hong Kong. One night we walked into an opium den by mistake. It was dark and smelled strange. We were greeted by hot and humid air with an odd sent of smoke almost like burnt clothes. All the old Chinese were on mats on the floor. Some were smoking long pipes while others were rolling their eyes back into their heads from the opium's effects.

The Chinese restaurants there were much different than home. I had duck one night. I had almost eaten the whole thing when a HKVDC [Hong Kong Volunteer Defence Corps] soldier told me how they cured it. They hung the duck outside by the neck until it rotted and dropped to the ground. They served the duck after it had rotted for days. Yuck. But it sure tasted good.

Around November 20, Andrew wrote, he went into Sham Shui Po for an evening visit where he went to several hotels with his buddies and had a few drinks at the Blue Lac. Before going home they went to a restaurant where he played poker for a monkey.

We played poker most nights, but not always for money. I won a monkey named Choko at a Chinese restaurant in town. Poor little bastard; he was going to be lunch if I lost. Monkey brain was quite a culinary treat in China in those days. The servers strapped a live monkey under the table with only the top of his head protruding through a hole in the centre. They would cut the top of the monkey's head off with a large machete, exposing his brain. The participants used chop sticks to eat the brains while the monkey was still alive. Culture shock got the best of me that night, so I proposed that we play poker for our dinner. When I won I unstrapped the monkey from under the table and took him with us back to the barracks. Choko was quite a hit around HQ Company. He got his name from his love for chocolate. He clung to me loyally, until someone offered him a chocolate, then he was gone to them. He came and went as he felt like it all day long, but usually at night he would find me.

For the next week the weather remained very hot. As part of their duties in HQ Company, Andrew and Ron issued supplies to the men like summer uniforms and sun helmets, and sent out the company laundry. They also checked equipment and weapons like mortar guns. "Ron told me the major wanted us to check the mortar guns. 'How do we check a mortar gun?' I asked. Ron shrugged his shoulders, so I checked one the Jacquet River way. As I dropped the mortar bomb in I caught sight of the major standing at the entrance of the building facing the parade ground. The mortar landed 100 feet from the major. Yep! The mortar gun worked and I was never asked to check one again."

Andrew was also kept busy supplying troops who were on duty outside of the camp, including at the regiment's battle stations on the southeast area of Hong Kong Island. They sent equipment to Tai Tam Gap, one of the island positions, for a company whose orders were to hold the post if they were attacked. Later on, Ron and Andrew, who were directed by the major to check out some of these positions, went out a few times to look at equipment and men at Tai Tam Gap.

The following week during training Andrew heard some encouraging details about the Japanese soldiers' weaknesses. They were told the Japanese couldn't see very well at night, because of the shape of their eyes. They also reportedly had limited military technology and fought on horseback with swords. It would be like shooting fish in a barrel, an English training officer told them. Andrew hoped the fellow was right. The officer also warned the Canadians about surrendering to the Japanese, stating that the Japanese Imperial Army soldiers would fall on their swords before being taken as prisoners. They believed being captured was a shameful act, punishable by death. The officer continued by asking, "So, what will they do to you if you surrender?" They'll show no mercy." "I thought by telling us this," Andrew said, "it was a great way to prevent any of us from giving up. With this knowledge, I assumed it was going to be a long fight, a fight to the end. We would fight until the last soldier fell." Andrew always concluded this part of his story with an absolutely sober tone.

Near the end of November, the situation became more serious. On the twenty-ninth Andrew heard that the Burma Road had been bombed by a Japanese air attack. On the thirtieth the Royal Rifles stood to all day and no one went into town that evening. They also got word that the Royal Scots Regiment was evacuated from the border to the north that day. English officers reportedly left the border commanded by a company sergeant-major.

On December 2, in what would be his last diary entry, Ron wrote that he had issued more supplies to the company. He also went over to Hong Kong bowling that evening. Andrew said, "I started writing diary entries after Ron stopped. I don't know why he stopped. Later Ron and I fought side by side in the Battle of Hong Kong. He was a ferocious fighter and a good friend."

Union Jack from Stanley Fort. AFC

Chapter Five

The Battle of Hong Kong

Each Christmas Andrew told his family the sad story of the Battle of Hong Kong. He didn't hold back on the particulars; perhaps his tongue was loosened by the beers he drank. He always spoke in great detail of the dialogue he and Joe Landry had the day they were captured. The narrative in this section draws on this conversation between the two soldiers.

On Christmas Day 1941, the Canadians stacked their weapons after receiving orders from the governor general of Hong Kong to surrender. They were in Stanley Fort, where Andrew saw the Union Jack on the ground being trampled by the Japanese. Later, when the guards were busy, Andrew picked up the flag that he had fought under and dusted off the dirt. He would say that a flag should never touch the ground, because it meant surrender, something he had no intention of doing. He folded the flag and rolled it tight, then placed it in his duffle bag. He kept the flag hidden throughout his long internment and flew it proudly when he got home as a reminder that he did not yield.

As Andrew sat huddled with a small group of friends, a crow soared overhead. Andrew envied his freedom! A feather fell from the bird, fluttering to the ground next to him. He pushed the sharp end of the plume into his breast pocket and shouted to the bird, "I'll give it back when I am as free as you are!"

The Japanese must have thought he was crazy, but his little friend Joe Landry knew exactly what he meant. Joe lived twenty miles from Andrew's home and had lied about his age to get in the army. They wished each other "Joyeux Noel" and then Joe asked Andrew if he thought the Japanese would shoot them.

When Andrew said he didn't know, Joe responded, "Did you hear what they did to two Hong Kong Volunteers when they tried to surrender? They run them through with bayonets, then cut off their privates and hung them on their faces." "They're bastards!" Andrew responded.

He knew Joe was scared. Joe was only fifteen, the same age as Andrew's brother Bud, who was safe at home. He hoped he could take care of Joe. At twenty-five Andrew was one of the older fellows there. "It's probably bull, Joe," Andrew tried to reassure his friend. "You know I won't let them hurt you. Remember the Jap on the hill that tried to run you through?"

"Yeah! He didn't see you coming," Joe responded.

"Exactly! The next one that screws with you won't see me neither," Andrew said with confidence.

Joe watched as Andrew took off one boot. When asked what he was doing, Andrew said, "See this page?" as he turned the piece of scribbler paper over. "Both sides are an account of what happened from December 6 until today. I'm hiding it in the lining of my boot so the guards won't take it. It's my diary of the Battle of Hong Kong."

When Joe asked him to read it, Andrew began with the first entry, dated December 6, 1941. He read how he had heard from a news dispatch that Japan would be at war with Great Britain and her allies, and also the United States of America, in the near future. "By the end of November the international press was freely speculating about an imminent Japanese offensive in South East Asia," he wrote.

Joe commented that Andrew hadn't written about the incident that day with their mascot Gander. Joe was referring to the incident at Sham Shui Po in the Royal Rifles barracks where some hungry Chinese people tried to lure Gander away. Their intention obviously was to serve the huge Newfoundland dog as their main course at dinner. Following a brief struggle, Gander had returned to his post in the shade on the veranda where he often slept. He seemed to develop a lasting distrust for all Asian people that day. Any Chinese worker on the base who came near where he lay would be ambushed. Indeed, one day he seized someone and would not let him go until a Canadian ordered him to release his victim. Andrew answered that he couldn't put that in; he had only had one page and it was full. He told Joe they wouldn't need a diary to remember Gander.

Joe accepted this explanation and asked what else Andrew had written. Andrew continued. By December 7, the Japanese appeared to be more aggressive and HQ Company was ordered to leave Kowloon and take up positions on the island of Hong Kong. They left Kowloon at approximately 1400 hours and arrived at Tai Tam Gap barracks about 1700 hours. That was also the day that Major MacAulay told Andrew that he would be his runner, relaying messages from one place to another and reporting back to the major. On December 8, they were up at 0430 hours. "Everyone was equipped for war, battle orders were given. We were at stand-to. At dawn the Battle for Hong Kong had begun," Andrew wrote. They soon heard that war had been declared. The Japanese bombed Kai Tak Airport and set fire to hangars, putting the airport out of commission. They also attacked Sham Shui Po with bombers.

The Canadians were up at 0430 hours again the next day. Bernard (Bunny) Duplassie and Andrew took up positions on the side of a ravine between Tai Tam Gap and Lye Mun (present-day Lei Yue Mun). They saw more bombs dropped on Lye Mun. "The Japanese also dropped propaganda bulletins asking the Chinese to join them against the English," Andrew wrote.

Andrew made three trips back and forth to HQ that day to report to Major MacAulay. "The major wasn't happy about the bombs or the propaganda," Andrew recorded.

On the tenth they heard about fierce fighting at the border. At 1000 hours the force commander, General Maltby, ordered the troops on mainland Hong Kong to prepare to evacuate.

The Japanese bombed Victoria on the western end of the island and broke through the Gin Drinkers Line. The next day it was rumoured that the Royal Scots and Punjab troops were retreating from the mainland border to take up positions on the island of Hong Kong.

For the next few days, they took up positions and saw Sai Wan bombed by the Japanese. Andrew noted that the Japanese were too far away to see

Japanese propaganda flyers, written in Chinese and English,
dropped during the Battle of Hong Kong. AFC

but he could smell the smoke and the bombers flew closer as the day went on. "Sometimes they were right above us, maybe 100 feet off the ground. We shot at the planes with our rifles when they were close." George S. MacDonell in *One Soldier's Story* recorded that on December thirteenth "a document signed by General Sakai (Japanese army), and sent across the harbour under a flag of truce requested the defenders to surrender to save further bloodshed. The request was refused categorically by the British governor, Sir Mark Young."

On the fourteenth Andrew got a bad scare when a shell burst in front of Tai Tam Gap barracks at 2000 hours, knocking the pots off the wall. Andrew recalled that Gander was outside, "but I think he slept through it. Nothing bothered Gander."

Rumour had it the next night that a large force of enemy tried to land at Pak Sha Wan, but they were successfully repulsed by the Canadians who inflicted heavy causalities on the Japanese. "The Japanese were probably just testing our defences...they came back with a vengeance the next day," Andrew recalled.

On the morning of the sixteenth Andrew and Duplassie went down to the China shack in front of headquarters for some lumber to make the blackout at the officers' mess more effective. It took them a half hour as they had to dodge about fifteen shells. As this was his first shelling in the open Andrew admitted that he was very scared. He considered scratching out "very scared" as "the enemy might think that I am afraid of them if they read that." The following day brought heavy shelling of the island from the mainland and more bombs fell on Shau Kei Wan, setting the city ablaze. On the eighteenth the shelling and bombing were the most severe, peaking around 2000 hours. The Japanese's full fury was centred on Shau Kei Wan and Lye Mun peninsula. About midnight they heard the enemy were landing troops once again at Shau Kei Wan.

On the nineteenth a heavy battle was fought around Mount Parker. Bert Roy, Alfie Miles, Corporal Robert L. Vincent, and quite a few more of Andrew's comrades were either captured or killed up there. Lieutenant Gerard Williams was killed that morning. Artillery opened up on the enemy who were on the eastern side of Mount Parker in front of Tai Tam

Gap headquarters. Around noon Andrew and HQ Company were ordered to go south to Palm Villa on Tai Tam Bay. Andrew left with some of Major MacAulay's equipment and returned to Tai Tam Gap at about 1600 hours where he got the major's trunk, bedroll, and knapsack along with his own kit bag and arrived back at Palm Villa about 2000 hours. He slept for short intervals in the truck in front of Palm Villa, and was up by 0400 hours.

Andrew had time to remember his fallen comrades. He recorded, "I liked Lieut. Williams; he was a good sort. Rest in Peace!" He also recorded that Sergeant-Major Robert Osborn of The Winnipeg Grenadiers "also died a heroic death up there."

He noted afterward that a Winnipeg Grenadier he met "told the guys that Osborn caught Japanese grenades bare-handed and hurled them right back. He said that the one Osborn didn't catch he jumped on, killing himself. He sacrificed himself to save his men." Osborn was posthumously awarded the Victoria Cross.

Gander also became a casualty early in the battle. According to Andrew:

> Joe Kelly [Gander's trainer or master] told me they were on the road close to Sai Wan Fort when they were ambushed by the Japanese. He said our troops jumped in the ditch and returned fire. Gander was guarding a few men who had been shot. The enemy hurled a grenade between the wounded lads. Gander picked up the grenade and ran off after them with it in his mouth. When the grenade exploded, Kelly said Gander probably took twenty or more Japanese with him. Kelly said it was the most heroic thing he'd ever saw a dog do.

Gander knew from watching the regiment train that a grenade was dangerous.

Andrew believed Gander should get a medal for saving those soldiers. In 2000, Gander posthumously received the Dickens Medal for sacrificing his own life to protect his comrades. The Dickens Medal is the animal equivalent to the Victoria Cross. Gander was the first Canadian animal to receive the honour. Andrew often said that upon hearing about Gander's demise he thought of that day on the river bridge when he saved Pup from drowning. Sadly, he would say, he knew that no amount of rope or brave deeds could bring Gander back. Word of Gander's final heroic deed spread quickly throughout the battlefield. His story was always told with the same honour and respect given to any fallen comrade. In his death Gander became a source of pride and encouragement for all the Canadians who eventually became POWs. He was their inspiration and the subject of many battle accounts.

At daybreak on the twentieth Andrew and several members of the company left to go to Repulse Bay, but they were held up on the way by intensive Japanese machine-gun fire. They took shelter in a small trench but when forced out they went up into the hills and then back to Palm Villa. During the encounter a bullet went through Andrew's knapsack. Earlier that day when they'd moved out, Andrew had been in charge of the major's trunk that was filled with his belongings, including four bottles of whisky. Andrew had to leave the trunk behind in the heat of the battle, but he removed the whisky and put it in his knapsack. He recalled, "The bullet broke two bottles of the major's B&B whisky. I don't know where his trunk ended up, but I got the rest of his whisky."

The next day, on December twenty-first, the company left at 0800 hours to launch an attack led by Major MacAulay from Palm Villa toward Tai Tam Tuk Reservoir. At a turn in the road by the petroleum dump they ran into about fifty Japanese soldiers. During the heavy battle that ensued, several Royal Rifle soldiers were killed and many wounded. As he went back to Palm Villa to get an ambulance, Andrew was sniped at a number of times by machine guns and rifles; a bullet gave him a flesh wound on his index finger. By the time he drove back with the ambulance to join the major, the Canadians had the enemy in full retreat. They moved on. As they came to the next turn an enemy car came racing toward them. The Canadians had two Bren gun carriers equipped with Vickers machine guns. The Vickers gunner opened up on the car and the enemy took into the woods. When Andrew and several other men pursued the enemy, the Japanese soldiers entered a house a short distance from where they abandoned their car. The Royal Rifles set their mortar into action. After the second round fired landed in the centre of the house, Andrew saw several Japanese soldiers running from behind the building toward the road that ran below the reservoir. Andrew and several Hong Kong Volunteers took up a position on the side of the road, and they were soon rewarded when several enemy soldiers tried to pass them. Andrew wrote that they won the firefight, although he later blacked it out in case the Japanese found his diary.

When Major MacAulay walked toward the abandoned car, he was hit by a sniper bullet, badly wounding his arm. A few minutes later Lieutenant Peters of the Hong Kong Volunteers was killed in the same place. When Andrew and several men got back to the turn by the petroleum dump, a Hong Kong Volunteer officer asked them to go up Red Hill where an enemy machine-gun nest was firing at their men on the other side of the high road. Andrew, Rifleman Ron Kinnie, Lance-Corporal Pollan, and several other soldiers advanced up the hill with fixed bayonets. After Kinnie got two of the enemy soldiers in the machine-gun nest with a Bren gun, the others retreated to the foot of the hill where they set fire to the hillside. About twenty minutes after the Canadians opened up on the machine-gun nest, they saw four enemy tanks coming from Tai Tam. When they were opposite the Canadians on the hill, the Japanese opened fire with machine guns, but none of the men were wounded. Andrew and the men came onto the highway below the turn in the road behind where the Japanese tanks were stopped. Kinnie took over an abandoned trench mortar truck, which he drove back to Palm Villa along with Private Ross and Andrew.

At 0500 hours on the twenty-second, Kinnie, Penichio, and Andrew took a Bren gun to a pillbox at Palm Villa. At 0900 hours they saw the enemy putting up mortars on top of nearby Bridge Hill. Sergeant Alfred Wonnacott took a platoon up to investigate. At 1100 hours Andrew and the others were ordered up Sugar Loaf Hill, which was opposite Bridge Hill in front of Palm Villa. At 1700 hours Andrew saw about three hundred enemy soldiers coming down the water catch toward Palm Villa. About thirty or forty Canadians, among them Kinnie with the Bren gun, ran back down the hill with fixed bayonets, and then charged up the water catch

Repulse Bay, December 1941. LAC PA-114819

where they turned the enemy back, running them to the top of Bridge Hill. Corporal Reginald Sommerville was killed in the charge and Corporal L.R. Latimer was killed in front of Palm Villa. At about 2100 hours, the Canadians came down from the hill, too late for supper. Andrew slept outside at South Cliff Villa until awakened by Sergeant W.R. Pope, who put Andrew on listening post by Palm Villa until 0300 hours. Andrew said he heard yapping dogs and the enemy up in the hills. He later recorded, "Sgt. Pope asked me where we lads from down home learned to fight. I told him there wasn't much else to do down home but fight and chase around in the woods. You know, in spite of the fear, I felt there was something familiar about the whole fighting affair."

Near the end of the Palm Villa battle Ron Kinnie, Fidele Legacy, Raymond Splude, Joe Landry, and Andrew were sleeping in a pillbox on the side of a hill. Andrew had not seen Choko the monkey for two weeks. Somehow, the little monkey found him in that pillbox. Andrew was asleep when Choko crawled in with him. He was exhausted when he awoke to something weighing heavily on his belly. Imagine his shock, two weeks into the battle with very little sleep, when he discovered something strange and hairy on his flesh. He whooped with fright. He apparently scared little Choko so badly that the monkey grabbed the closest things he could get a handle on and squeezed real tight. Andrew jumped straight up, screaming in agony at Choko's tight grip on his testicles. That was the last time Andrew saw little Choko. Afterward, Andrew often wondered aloud about the monkey's fate.

On the twenty-third, fierce machine-gun fire came from around South Cliff along with many snipers. Andrew saw enemy soldiers with machine guns all over Bridge Hill. The Canadians soon retreated south to Stanley View where Andrew slept outside in the rain. Late on Christmas Eve they fell back into Stanley Fort, the most southerly point on the island. Professor Endacott writes in *Hong Kong Eclipse* that on Christmas Eve "the Royal Rifles which had borne the brunt of the attacks in the east for five days and needed rest were withdrawn into Stanley Fort." But they came under heavy machine-gun fire all the way up to the fort. Andrew said they were backed into a corner, with no other place to retreat.

Andrew's final entry for the battle, written on December 25, reads: "Brigade headquarters shelled all day, counted 1008 shells. Kinnie was killed at 1700 hours. At 2000 hours we were told that the Governor of Hong Kong had surrendered the island." Indeed, his friend Ron Kinnie was killed in the final three hours of the battle. Kinnie had gone in with another company to clean up what was reported to be only fifteen Japanese in a house just outside of Fort Stanley. When the company got to the house there were hundreds of Japanese soldiers there, preparing for their final assault on the fort. Many Canadians were killed or wounded at that last fight, including Ron.

Shortly afterward the Canadians surrendered and they entered a new phase of their endless battle as prisoners of war.

Chapter Six

POWs at Hong Kong

By Boxing Day 1941, all the Canadian soldiers had heard that Hong Kong had surrendered. As they stacked their weapons everyone wore a look of shock, like they were in pain. That afternoon the Japanese buzzed around Stanley Fort like a swarm of hornets whose nest had been kicked, angry and eager to sting or hurt. In spite of their victory, they didn't seem to be well organized. Months later Andrew found out from a guard that the Japanese had never intended or planned to keep prisoners. To the Japanese, surrender was dishonourable. Andrew surmised that they thought they would just kill all of the captured Allies, or maybe they assumed the Allies would commit *hara-kiri* (suicide), as they might have done if the circumstances had been reversed.

Most of the Canadian soldiers were out of rations and were hungry. The Japanese finally gave them some food in the evening. Andrew stood in line with Fidele Legacy for a few hours just to get a rusty pot and a small quantity of rice; there was no meat or vegetables. Andrew said he didn't realize, at that point in their incarceration, how much he would grow to hate rice. Fidele and Andrew boiled the rice over a charcoal fire and portioned it out. They each had about three ounces. Wondering what they were eating at home that night, Andrew concluded that he would never again complain about leftovers. Unlike Andrew who was a lightweight and never had a big appetite, Fidele was a large man weighing over 200 pounds. The meagre ration wouldn't stave off his hunger. For the second night as POWs they slept outside.

The next day they were up before sunrise and had to march several miles before they came to a bombed-out area. On the way Andrew puked

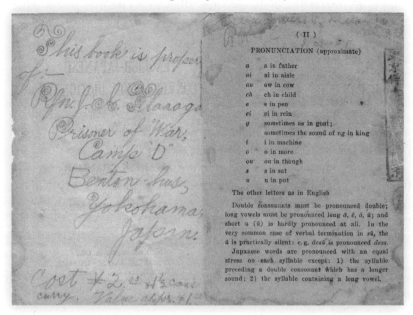

(III)

PREFIXES.

o	honorific
ō	big; great
ko	small; young of animals
go	honorific
o	male
me	female

SUFFIXES.

ka	means interrogation or doubt
na	added to noun to form adj.
ni	added to noun to form adverb
ya	shops; occupation of workmen
mono	concrete noun
koto	abstract noun
sa	added to adj. forms an abstract noun
gata	plural (polite)
tachi	plural
domo	plural (less polite)

CONTRACTIONS.

da = de aru	*desū = de arimasū*
datta = de atta	*deshita = de arimashita*
darō = de arō	*deshō = de arimashō*
ja = de wa	

ya = wa after indefinite form of the verb (2nd base)
e.g. *shi ya shi-nai*
cha = te wa; e.g. *shicha = shite wa*
chau = te shimau; e.g. *wasurechau*
chatta = te shimatta e.g. *wasurechatta*
mon = mono
nan = nani
te = to itte mo; to iu; to itta

¥3.

ENGLISH-JAPANESE CONVERSATION DICTIONARY

PRECEDED BY A FEW

ELEMENTARY NOTIONS

OF

JAPANESE GRAMMAR

COMPILED BY

ARTHUR ROSE-INNES

REVISED EDITION

K. Yoshikawa & Co.,
BOOKSELLERS AND STATIONERS,
No. 5, Benten-dori, Yokohama.
(All rights reserved.)

Andrew's English-Japanese dictionary. AFC

This book is properof :—

Rfn: J. A. E. Slanoga

Prisoner of War;

Camp "D"

Benton hu,

Yokohama,

Japan.

Cost ¥2.⁰⁰ 4½ cents
carry. Value appr. ¥1.²⁰

(II)

PRONUNCIATION (approximate)

a	a in father
ai	ai in aisle
au	ow in cow
ch	ch in child
e	e in pen
ei	ei in rein
g	sometimes as in goat; sometimes the sound of ng in king
i	i in machine
o	o in more
ou	ou in though
s	s in sat
u	u in put

The other letters as in English

Double consonants must be pronounced double; long vowels must be pronounced long *ā, ē, ō, ū;* and short *u (ŭ)* is hardly pronounced at all. In the very common case of verbal termination in *sŭ,* the *ŭ* is practically silent: e.g. *desŭ* is pronounced *dess.*
Japanese words are pronounced with an equal stress on each syllable except: 1) the syllable preceding a double consonant which has a longer sound; 2) the syllable containing a long vowel.

twice from hunger; he only managed to get a spit of bile out of his empty belly each time. They worked hard all day putting barbwire fencing around a half dozen shacks near an old airstrip, stopping work at dark. There were several hundred prisoners in that camp, mostly Canadian and Indian soldiers. Eventually, the POWs were relocated to North Point Camp overlooking Victoria Harbour. Andrew stayed there until he was transferred to Camp Sham Shui Po in August, where he remained until January 1943.

The Japanese set up a mess area outside where the POWs cooked rice in rusty barrels. The rice tasted like metal, but Andrew was so hungry he ate it anyway. The portions were minuscule. When one fellow was caught trying to get seconds, several Japanese guards beat him brutally. The sound of each blow sickened Andrew. The fellow lay on the ground for all to see and his friends were not allowed to move him. They buried him behind the latrines the following morning.

The next day the POWs ate the leftover cold rice, and the portions were even smaller. Andrew met Raj, an Indian soldier from the Punjab troops. Andrew would say that he couldn't pronounce his last name. Like Andrew, Raj was thin; he assumed Andrew had been deprived of food at home. When Raj remarked that back in India they didn't have much to eat *just like the Canadians*, Andrew didn't have the heart to tell him that he lived on a farm and had never gone hungry a day in his life.

Working and studying with Dr. Smith had taught Andrew the importance of communication. He got an English-Japanese dictionary by trading a guard one can of curry plus ¥2 (two yen). Andrew had acquired the can of curry by unethical means, as the Japanese would put it, when it had fallen out of a guard's knapsack right in front of Andrew. "I scooped up the can of curry like a kingfisher on a mackerel. I tied the can inside my drawers and walked around all day with that can banging on my nuts. I was determined to learn Japanese, so when a Jap guard showed me the dictionary, I offered him the curry. He took the can and wrote '¥2' in the dirt. I gave him the last change I had in my pocket then he passed me the book."

When the Japanese told the POWs to eat the same leftover rice that they had cooked three days earlier, they scraped the bottoms of the barrels and divided up the scraps. "Thank God it was dark," Andrew said. "The portion was tiny, but it had more protein. I could feel something wiggle in my mouth. In time I got used to eating maggots."

New Year's Day had a whole new meaning, according to Andrew, when he was a POW. What possible resolution could he make? Perhaps he could vow to eat more and get kicked around less. But it wouldn't matter because he had no control over either. Andrew hoped this would be his only New Year as a POW. The POWs received new rice and some greens to make soup with, which helped to cheer the boys up.

The Japanese were disorganized and didn't know what to do with the POWs. Andrew said they had one English language book in camp, *Gone with the Wind*, and they each took turns reading it. Life became boring and mundane. Days ran into weeks, and before he knew it, months had passed. Each day brought more of the same, mostly starvation. Some days they were fed twice, others three times, but always rice.

By March they were being used as slave labourers to reconstruct the bombed-out Kai Tak Airport on Kowloon Bay. They worked very hard, for long hours. The Japanese gave them Sundays off from work duty. Andrew said for the most part he was too tired or too sore to do much. Many fellows were dying. Some days they held three funerals.

The POWs lived in filth. They were infested with head and body lice, and bedbugs were everywhere. "On Sundays," Andrew explained, "I washed my meagre belongings, including the rags on my bed. After I killed the bedbugs I put boot grease on the bed posts to try to prevent them from climbing back up in my bed. It wasn't much of a bed; just a wooden bunk with a few jute bags for blankets. Woollen blankets were few and far between."

The men in the camp made a vow to keep rank and they refused to salute the Japanese guards. They washed their clothes and shaved like they were back in basic camp as a show of their resilience. Washing helped to control the lice and other parasites.

Even though they were exhausted from work, hunger, and beatings, the POWs gave their dead a decent send-off. "I and many other POWs got beaten often," Andrew said. "A Jap threw a sledge hammer at me one day; I was lucky, only the wooden handle hit my head. The Japs slapped my face to humiliate me many times; they knew I couldn't hit them back. That robbed me of my dignity. I wasn't very big, and to be honest I was used to coming in second in most fights back home, but I could always hit back. That frustration got replaced with hatred for the bastards that beat on me. I survived knowing that someday the war would be over and it would be my turn to hit." His stare grew cold as he thought back on the experience.

Several men in Andrew's shack died over the winter, mostly from infection in wounds they had received in battle or from beatings in the camp. Bud Sweet from Bathurst, Leo Pitre from Culligans, and Fred Elsliger from Jacquet River were in his shack. Bud was lucky to be alive; during the battle he'd been machine gunned and was being treated at St. Stephen's College hospital when the Japanese went on their murderous campaign. He was bayonetted in the arm as he lay helpless in his bed. His arm had had to be amputated because it became infected, but at least he was alive.

The atrocities at St. Stephen's College were well known among the Canadian POWs. A young soldier from Quebec who was in Andrew's shack had witnessed the slaughter. He saw the Japanese killing wounded, defenceless patients in their beds. He said one officer, who had apparently lost a brother in the battle, was exceptionally cruel to the wounded Canadians. Among them was a soldier from Andrew's hometown, John McKay, who was only twenty-two years old. John was dragged out of his bed to the corridor where the Japanese cut off his ears and cut out his tongue, according to the young Quebec soldier. They laughed and kicked at him until he finally died from their brutality. The Japanese soldiers also raped and mutilated the nurses and butchered many others on Christmas Day. A doctor who tried to stop the madness had his throat slit by the attackers.

Lying in bed, too cold, hungry, and sore to sleep, Andrew often thought about home. To entertain himself he pretended to listen in on his family's conversations. It made him feel closer to them. Andrew wondered what his mother and father knew. He figured they wouldn't know if he was alive or dead, and he hoped that they didn't worry too much.

Andrew and Fred Elsliger worked together a lot. When the Japanese were not around they talked. The conversation was always about home, where they wished they could be again. Fred talked about the fun he had with his siblings. "I missed my brothers and sister too," Andrew recalled.

A Japanese guard gave Fred and Andrew each a shovel and a bucket, and pointed to the latrine area where the outhouse facilities were filled with raw sewage. Back home when the facilities were too full they buried the hole with gravel and dug a new one, but not here. The guard ran over to them as they began digging a fresh hole, yelling, "*Yama!*" (Stop!). He grabbed the bucket and shoved Andrew's head in it as he shouted orders in Japanese. "Thank God it was empty," Andrew would say as he told the story. The guard indicated that he wanted them to fill the buckets with the sewage and empty the contents into barrels.

As Andrew worked at the job he remembered something Dr. Smith had told him. Upon retiring as headmaster of Bishop's College School, Smith walked many beaches throughout the Maritimes in search of the perfect building lot. In Prince Edward Island he admired a house overlooking the Northumberland Strait. He inquired as to who lived in that beautiful home.

"Oh, that's proud MacDonnell," a local man replied.

"Why do you refer to him as proud MacDonnell?" Smith asked.

"Because he shits in a box," the Islander said, shaking his head with disdain.

"Apparently, proud MacDonnell had a flushable lavatory." Smith would chuckle as he ended the story.

Andrew and Fred repeated the stinking task all afternoon until the latrine holes were empty and all the barrels were full. Andrew found out later that the Japanese used the human excrement as fertilizer for their vegetable gardens.

On March 2, 1942, Andrew recorded that he and fellow POWs were working harder than ever. "The guards are beating guys that can't keep up. I am sure they killed a coolie. Poor bastard; the Japs hated the Chinese."

On that day Andrew was working with Joe Landry. Andrew recalled part of their conversation. "That looks like a dead body on the floor of the quarry, Joe," Andrew said.

"It's the coolie that carries the water. The Jap guard said she fell off the cliff, you know the one that beats them all the time," Joe replied. They smelled the corpse for over a month every time the wind blew across the quarry. "Believe me, rotting humans stink! It was an extremely pungent smell and it sickened my empty stomach."

While Andrew endured his hardships as a POW, his parents struggled with his loss at home. Andrew later recalled a lengthy story that started before he became a POW, about assigning his pay. The day he learned he would soon ship out Andrew requested that the paymaster in Valcartier assign $20 from his pay to his father. Andrew also wrote to his mother telling her she must take the $20 each month to Stewart McAlister to make his car payment. As a POW in 1942, Andrew had no idea that his parents were not being treated the way a soldier's family should. The army didn't want to pay his father. Andrew's family believed the army may have thought he was dead. The army was probably worried that if he were dead they might never collect the advanced amounts. Frustrated, Andrew's father wrote to the army, which forwarded his letters to the Dependants' Allowance Board. Andrew's folks kept copies of the correspondence including many letters concerning the assignment of his pay, which documented his family's fight on the home front. Among them was a letter from Andrew's father written during his captivity.

The Secretary,
Dept. National Defence,
Assigned Pay Branch
Ottawa Can.

March 1, 1942
Dear Sir:

Before my son left Canada for Hong Kong he informed me

that he assigned $20.00 of his monthly pay to me. He said that I could expect the first cheque the latter part of October /41, but so far I have not received any amount from the Dept. I am very anxious about this matter as I was to settle a monthly obligation of his and I cannot do so unless I receive the money. I give you below his regiment number, rank and name. Please let me hear about this matter.

Yours & only,
James Flanagan
Jacquet River, N.B.

Later in life Andrew said he was glad that he didn't know about the problem. "Imagine, me away fighting for my country and the folks unable to make my payment. They would be devastated." Andrew's father would have been hard pressed to make the back payments from his own resources. Money was very tight for Andrew's parents. His father operated a small mixed farm, which generated little revenue. His mother's schoolteacher pay was used for living expenses. His family could not afford to make his car payments on their own.

Early in April 1942 the Deputy Judge Advocate General agreed with their claim and advised the director of pay services to make the assignment pay if and when supporting letters and affidavits were received from his parents. His mother's affidavit read:

I solemnly swear that my son, E30353, J. Andrew Flanagan, Rifleman, Royal Rifles of Canada, wrote to me telling me that he had assigned twenty dollars ($20.) of his monthly pay to his father and that he could expect the first payment either in October or November 1941.

(Signed) Mrs. Mary E. Flanagan
(Mother of above soldier)

Sworn to before me
This 10th day of April 1942,
Bert Roherty, J.P. Armstrong Brook, N.B.

Finally, in a letter to Andrew's parents dated April 12, 1942, the army agreed to the assignment.

Dear Sir:

Assigned Pay E.30353 Rfm. Flanagan, J.A.
Your letter of April 10th has been received enclosing sworn declaration of Mrs. Mary E. Flanagan and you are advised that an assignment of $20.00 per month payable to you and effective from January 1st 1942 has been put in force. You will receive an adjustment cheque in due course.

In a follow-up letter Andrew's father asked for the other two months' back pay, representing November and December. However, his father received a letter from a paymaster declining his request. By June 1942, the twenty-dollar assignment cheques were being paid but with no back pay. The army sent his father the money until December 1945. Andrew learned after the war that upon hearing about the army's refusal to pay the back payments, Dr. Smith had brought the account up to date, giving Stewart McAlister strict orders to keep it anonymous.

In the meantime, Andrew's folks didn't know if he was alive or dead. They couldn't get any information from the army so they asked Dr. Smith to write to his friend Colonel Clarke for information. Clarke was also one of Dr. Smith's former students at Bishop's College School.

Dr. Smith, as an Oxford man, was revered in the local community as a notable scribe. He often helped locals with their correspondence. One fellow asked Dr. Smith to write to a government department requesting help with a local road repair. The fellow bragged at the post office about how Smith told the department off. But when asked what Smith had written, the fellow had to admit he didn't know because he couldn't understand the words Smith used, "but it sure sounded good."

Dr. Smith helped Andrew's family by writing the following abridged letter.

September 5, 1942
My dear Colonel Clarke:

I am much interested in E 30353 Rfn. Flanagan, James Andrew, who was Major MacAulay's batman. Before enlisting in the Royal Rifles he had lived with me as a cook for seven years & his parents are my nearest neighbours. They have from time to time shown me the kind letters they have received from you & you will readily believe that they are deeply disappointed in receiving no letters from Hong Kong. I may add that they have three sons in the Canadian Army in England.

Any help you may give in this matter will be deeply appreciated by Flanagan's parents.

I have some idea of the anxiety his parents must have felt ever since last Christmas; for in seven years I had become much attached to Flanagan, & I have longed to hear that he was well or alive.

With kindest regards to you, Mrs. Clarke & your boys.

Yours very sincerely, Stephen Percy Smith

By September 9, 1942, Colonel Clarke had written back to Smith.

I appreciate your anxiety to learn more of Rifleman James Andrew Flanagan, whose parents did not receive a letter from him. I wrote to Mr. James Flanagan on September 3, and my letter probably crossed yours of September 5th. In my letter I explained that parents and relatives must not take the failure to receive a letter as an indication that the soldier has not survived the battle of Hong Kong.

On October 31, Andrew's father received the following cable confirming that he was alive.

October 27, 1942
Department of National Defence –
ARMY

The following extract from a cable received from the International Red Cross Committee, Geneva, is forwarded for your information.

Reg. No E-30353.................. Rank Rfmn..................
Name FLANAGAN.......James.....Andrew...
Unit The Royal Rifles of Canada (Ca)...................
Nature of Report Tokyo cables Prisoner of War at a Hong Kong Camp
Next of Kin James Flanagan......................
Relationship Father...........................
Address Jacquet River, Restigouche Co. N.B..........

Back in Hong Kong, after months as a POW, Andrew was ready to escape. Early on, there had been several successful escapes to China, but in June 1942 General Maltby had issued orders that there would be no more individual or small group escapes. Andrew wrote, "On 21st June signed off declaration not to escape, won't stop me from bugging off if the opportunity presents itself. No chance, no use, suicide to try." He said later that he would have walked away whistling Dixie, if given the opportunity. "I was probably lucky I didn't get a chance. I heard of a few Grenadiers who escaped. They were recaptured and executed on the spot." Oliver Lindsay writes in *The Battle for Hong Kong 1941-1945: Hostage to Fortune* that "on August 20th four brave men from the Winnipeg Grenadiers escaped from

North Point Camp. Their sampan sank when they were trying to cross to the mainland. They were picked up by the Japanese Navy, beaten with baseball bats and then shot without trial."

Near the end of August, Andrew wrote that no one had received news from home. When the camp captain asked if they could write letters home, Andrew said, he got a beating. In October, the Japanese guards took Andrew's diary from December 26, 1941, to October 11, 1942. They wanted to review its content. Andrew said he asked the guard for it back but never saw it again. He assumed correctly that the Japanese didn't like the fact that he wrote about the hunger and cruelty he and his fellow POWs suffered.

"I had lost it all, but I would remember everything. At that point I was glad that I had hidden the Battle of Hong Kong in the lining of my boot; they couldn't take what they didn't know existed. The lesson I learned that day was to keep my diaries, but to be careful about how I worded events and our treatment."

The next day Andrew recorded in a new notebook that the boys were dying like flies, with dip (diphtheria), some days three. The next sentence was blacked out. Sometimes during reviews the guards would black out things that they didn't want him writing about, and other times he would black out items that might get him or his friends in trouble. Mid-month Andrew pondered his existence, writing, "We live in hope, though we may die in despair. JAF."

In late October, Andrew said, the Japanese became very angry one day. The first heavy military plane had landed on the new airstrip that the POWs had built. Andrew and his fellow POWs watched the plane circle and come in for the landing. As it touched down, dust and smoke from the wheels enveloped the plane. A puff of wind cleared their line of sight. They saw the plane skid to a stop on its belly without its wheels. When the plane hit the tarmac, it had sunk over a foot into the airstrip, clipping its wheels off.

Andrew admitted he thought the Japanese were going to seek revenge on the POWs, but they blamed their engineer who was supposed to be in charge of the project. Apparently, the Japanese engineer felt that project was beneath him, so he'd assigned an English civil engineer to do the work. The Englishman was very smart, knowing exactly how to build a deficient airstrip. After that incident the POWs' war was fought with sabotage whenever they got the chance. As night fell the Japanese engineer was brought out to the parade ground where he was beheaded by his comrades in front of the POWs. "Japs killing Japs, now that was more like it!" Andrew later recalled.

The next day, Andrew said, he got a beating when one of the Japanese civilians on his shift told the guards that he was laughing and poking fun at the Japanese who were trying to fix the airstrip. "It was hard not to laugh at the arrogant bastards," Andrew would say. He got a few big welts on his back where the guard had struck him several times with the flat side of his sword. Most times when he was taking a beating from the Japanese he would imagine boxing with the guard where he would be able to hit back. It was one of the ways he coped. Andrew concluded that he'd have loved to have had that Japanese guard between the house and barn back home. It would have been a fight that his father would have enjoyed.

Andrew explained, "Pop picked up a couple of old pairs of boxing gloves for us. The boxing provided endless entertainment for him and the family. Pop loved to watch us boys box, but he got the biggest kick watching my sister Rita go blow for blow with any boy around home."

Andrew recorded the passing of his friends. He wrote that by Halloween that year Bob Barclay had been buried. The funeral service was held at 0100 hours in the St. Francis chapel Sham Shui Po POW Camp and he was buried at 1500 hours in the Argyle Prisoner Cemetery. The pallbearers were Mac (Phil) Gallie, Gerald Hachey, Francis Robertson, and Andrew himself. Bob Barclay was from Jacquet River and "his people owned and operated the Barclay Hotel in front of the old liquor store (Frenette's), just beyond the Rail Road crossing," Andrew recalled.

Early in November 1942 Andrew wrote that he finally found out the whereabouts of the personal belongings of his deceased friend Ron Kinnie. Captain Everette Ernest Denison had them. He gave them to Andrew who said he would get them to Canada if possible. On November 2, "the personal articles Ron had on him, on Xmas day last, & which he wanted

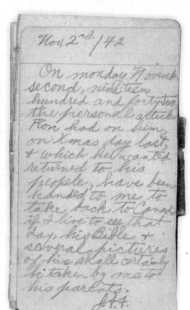

Andrew's diaries. AFC

returned to his people, have been handed to me to take back to Canada if I live to see that day, his Bible & several pictures of his shall certainly be taken by me to his parents. J.A.F."

Later, Andrew said that while sitting on his bunk, he felt a lump in his throat as he examined the contents of Ron's belongings. Among them was a picture in a celluloid plastic protector, darkened with Ron's own dried brown blood, which sealed the picture in place. Andrew didn't think he could give the picture to Ron's mother. "I felt Ron's soul on that blood-stained picture. I missed Ron. My only regret was that I didn't have more time to get to know him. I dreamt about him sometimes. In my dreams I always knew he was dead, but we talked casually, like we were in heaven and were just having a chat."

Another good friend of Andrew's was Paul Dallain, whose hometown was New Carlisle, Quebec. "Paul was finally put in the camp hospital today," Andrew wrote. "He was very feverish." He predicted that Paul would have a hard time pulling through, but Andrew vowed to help his friend any way that he could. He gave cigarette butts and anything else he could scrounge to help Paul and his other sick friends. "So many go into the hospital, but too many come out feet-first, dead. I hope Paul pulls through," Andrew wrote.

One day in mid-November, he wrote that he was working indoors with the ration party and that he received ¥1 from the camp command. "Inside was a rest for a change. I handled onions, sweet potatoes & radish." Andrew later said that they would do what was necessary to get food, including stealing from the Japanese, but if they were caught there would be hell to pay.

The next day Andrew was back at hard work joining a working party at Kai Tak Airport. He had a good day because the bosses couldn't get the diesel engines going, so he did nothing all day. By then, many POWs had a disease called *wet beriberi*, caused by thiamine deficiency, and Andrew was worried he might be getting *dry beriberi*. His feet were sore and he started to do the "beriberi shuffle"—that's what the POWs called the gait of the afflicted lads. Andrew knew he needed rice husks, since the white polished rice had no vitamins, according to the camp doctor. He said his feet felt like little electric shocks ran through them when he took a step. He knew it would get worse if he didn't get vitamins. Walking back to camp Andrew was cheered to see white people on a ship—they were mostly Portuguese—which reminded him of home. He also said that he could have escaped because there were no Japanese guards along the way, but where would he have gone? And who would take care of Paul Dallain and the others? He said he thought it over and decided that the time wasn't right. On November 16, 1942, Andrew wrote, "One year ago today we stepped foot in China. I wonder when we will leave this God forsaken country. I wish it would be soon, but if soon I imagine it will be feet-first, to cross the Jordan instead of the Pacific."

Andrew and his friend Vic managed to find some "S.P." (sweet potatoes) that they "slunged" on for a week. (A slunge or slunger was POW slang for a scoff or surprise lunch.) The Japanese didn't cook for them, thank God, Andrew recalled. Because he had cooked for Dr. Smith, the camp command assigned him as a cook. It was just as well because he could hardly stand because of the beriberi. In his search for a remedy he ate husks, wild plants, and roots when he could find them. "I am feeling a lot better," he wrote. "We trade the Japanese cigarettes for food items like sugar, M & V [meat and vegetables] and salt fish."

As cook Andrew kept a notebook with recipes. The front of the book read, "Cooking Recipes junked up in a Prisoner of war camp, from troops." Andrew asked his fellow POWs to write their favourite recipes in the cookbook. When the cooks had some ingredients on hand that were similar to those for one of the recipes listed, they'd cook them up and call the dish by a title like *jam fritters*, which were "thin bread sandwiches, dipped in flour batter & fried in deep fat." This was a Jamaican treat, picked up by one of the Winnipeg Grenadiers who was stationed there before Hong Kong, Andrew said later as he looked through the recipe book.

The cookbook contained an international menu. Prisoners from different cultures, countries, and experiences wrote their best recipes, such as:

Kagkoe Joe's cheese cakes (Soviet): "Mix flour and grated cheese in equal proportions, add pinch salt. Roll out to 1 inch thick, bake hot oven."

Comvloa (Norwegian): "Equal parts grated raw potatoes and flour. 4 cups milk, 1 tsp. salt, mix and form into dumplings, cook in meat broth for 20 mins. Keep lid closed tight."

To keep up morale even when the cooks couldn't find any of the ingredients, they would name most meals from one of the titles in the cookbook. On many nights rice became "paté du jour."

Andrew's diaries recorded much discussion about food, weather, and POW obituaries. On November 20, he wrote, "Very wet, up @ 0430 to feed the officers. I am going on work party today. Vic & I had a big slunge of smuggled S.P. It was swell. Bert Sweetman died of dysentery." One day he got a surprise in his watered-down soup when he found a piece of a horse lip in his broth; it was hard to chew, but it was meat. He didn't want to

A page from Andrew's
recipe book. AFC

Peanut Butter Mixture.

5 lbs. peanuts.
1 " Butter.
2 " Syrup or honey.
Heat butter & syrup, mix
in peanuts & butter, add
walnuts or pecans if
you desire.

swallow it because he wanted
to savour the taste for as long
as he could. He chewed on it
all day.

Andrew also recorded how
he tried to help his mates. One
day he bought an egg and gave
it to Paul Dallain, who was very weak and still in the hospital. The next day
he gave Paul a pack of cigarettes and a pound of sugar. "He's to be admired
for his fighting spirit, but I don't think he would make it," Andrew wrote.
Another day Andrew gave Paul a fruit cake and he looked a little stronger.
Andrew was doing his best to keep Paul alive until he got the chance to go
to Bowing Road, a real hospital off camp. At the end of November, after
Paul had gone to Bowing Road Hospital, Andrew wrote that his friend
had an excellent chance for survival there with the proper treatment and
that Paul was getting a little stronger all that week.

On Tuesday, November 24, Andrew wrote that Rifleman Arthur
McAllister had died at 0300 hrs. Andrew was on stand-to for his funeral.
The service was held at church by Captain Strong, R.N., at 1500 hours.
"Art had no hope of getting back to Canada," Andrew wrote. "From the first
time he was taken prisoner he had electric feet, then cholera. Dysentery
got him. The day before he expired he got out of bed & said he was going
to fool us all by living." Later Andrew would say, "Arthur was from Nash
Creek, NB. He was a hell of a nice fellow and a good man. I knew him
most of my life."

As for Andrew's health, he was still fending off beriberi. He was not
as sore, which he attributed to eating the husks and weeds, and also to
helping Paul. That same day, the twenty-fourth, he wrote that he worked

at Kai Tak Airport again as driver on the train. The train was a gravity-fed railed dump-car system. The cars were filled with rocks and gravel at the quarry then driven downhill to the airport site. Once they were unloaded, a fixed diesel engine pulled the carts back up the hill to the quarry. He also got four cigarettes that day. And he recorded that Gerald Hachey from Bathurst was in the camp hospital. "Hope he makes it."

The next day he recorded that he was again at Kai Tak as driver on the train. "Full speed ahead," he wrote. "Got 3 fags," which was followed by, blacked out but legible, "Over thirty planes on the field. I heard of bombing by allies, told to me by a Portuguese."

"Cigarettes were more valuable than money, trumped only by food of course," Andrew would say. He traded cigarettes and butts for just about anything, especially food. The Japanese were generally poor and they traded a lot. The guards sometimes flicked their cigarette butts into a can, which Andrew raided every chance he got. The third most valuable trading items were pictures from home or from any place outside of the camp. "When I held a picture of any place beyond the camp I would imagine being there. It was a way to escape in my mind," Andrew concluded.

At the end of November, Andrew got his first Red Cross package. It was a happy day in camp. He put most of his stuff away until Christmas. "With regards to the Red Cross parcels we sure had to wait a heck of a long time to get them, but we sure welcome them now when our rations are so low, as rice only isn't much, & so many suffering from malnutrition [something here was blacked out] to see the boys on parade one would think by the amount of cripples hobbling along that they were bound for St. Anne de Beaupre. JAF 30-11-42."

While telling that story Andrew remarked that the substance in the parcel wasn't as important as the hope it afforded. He stored the contents at the head of his bunk. He knew no one would touch it. There was a code in the camp where they shared everything but a man would starve to death before he would take another fellow's food.

According to Andrew, the Japanese had kept most of the previous Red Cross packages. One time they gave the POWs Red Cross razor blades after the guards had worn them out shaving.

The Red Cross also sent real food like bacon and eggs for supper, as well as meat and vegetables. Andrew wrote that they had a slunger.

The first week of December was very cold. Working outside at Kai Tak was bone chilling, according to Andrew. "Worked like slaves. No. 1 said he'd report me to [something blacked out] for not working hard enough. I told him there would be some reporting done to the British when we take back Hong Kong." Number 1, Andrew's Japanese boss, was bad for reporting the POWs to their commander, who would beat them.

Rumours were always circulating around the workplace. A Chinese worker who was a tailor by trade told Andrew that the Chinese would take back Hong Kong within twenty-four days. Andrew said he wished he was optimistic enough to believe him.

At the end of the first week of December Andrew was still working at the airport where he sent fifteen dump cars on line No. 6 down from the quarry to the construction site.

In 1990, as Andrew was reading his diaries aloud, he stopped at this section to tell a brief story about the entertainment they made for themselves as POW slave labourers. "I worked on a hill in the quarry. Narrow-gauge wood rail tracks carried my car loads of gravel by gravity to the worksite. The cars were old, about four feet by ten feet, mostly wood on an iron frame, with a long wooden friction brake. Two of us jumped on it and wow, down we went. I didn't put the brake on until the last minute. We run the car arse over kettle, both of us flew through the air. The hardest part was putting it back on the track."

Andrew said he heard that Frank Method broke his ankle on one of these rides. Frank was a First Nations soldier from the Restigouche reserve in Quebec. There were a number of Aboriginals with Andrew, including a good friend named Pat Matalic. "They were all good fellows and were fearless fighters in the Battle of Hong Kong," Andrew said. "Since the battle, I had a whole new respect for the term Indian Brave."

On December 7, Andrew wrote his usual entries, like the fact that it was very cold in the early morning, but it warmed in the afternoon; they were also issued a Red Cross sweater, two pairs of underwear, and a pair of socks. He later pointed to a blacked-out section of his diary and said that a Japanese guard had ripped the bottom of the page out because he didn't like what he wrote. Andrew said he had written, "The Japs are keeping the best Red Cross stuff for their own troops." The Japanese regularly inspected and censored his diary. They blackened entries or ripped pages out if it made them look bad. Sometimes Andrew had to blacken out intimidating words, phases, or sections. He couldn't write about the beatings, starvation, or forced labour without getting into trouble. "The hell with that, I wrote about it anyway," Andrew said defiantly.

On December 8, Andrew recorded, "A black day, one year ago war started here." In December they were still working at Kai Tak Airport where the Kamloops Kid kept their noses to the grindstone. Although they sent down fifteen cars a shift, the Kid said they weren't working hard enough. Once again, the bottom of the page in his diary was torn out. The Kamloops Kid was a second-generation Japanese-Canadian who was born and raised in Kamloops, BC, and spoke perfect English. "The Canadian POWs considered the Kamloops Kid a traitor and in my mind he justified the internment of Japanese Canadians back home," Andrew said.

Andrew's first encounter with the Kid was in Sham Shui Po where he was the interpreter in charge of the Canadian POWs. He was one of the cruellest Japanese guards Andrew ever ran across. "He hit me or any other prisoner with anything he had in hand; staff, gun, or even tools. He beat several POWs to death." When the war was over, Andrew hoped to stay behind and help catch the Kid. "You know he'd get his up and comings if I caught him," a steel-faced Andrew would say.

The Kid ripped the bottom of the page that Andrew had pointed out.

He was pissed that Number 1 told me the Kid hated Canadians because they teased him growing up. He demanded an apology; I wouldn't. I hated the son of a bitch. That day, he gave me a pile-driver to the gut. I was ordered to stand at attention while he beat me with a bamboo stick until I fell down. If I hit him back, the Japs would have killed me. When I hollered in pain he hit me harder. It was not so much the physical pain that bothered me; it was the humiliation and embarrassment of not being able to fight back.

Andrew went on to explain that his general strategy for surviving a beating consisted of a screwed-up system of prayer and cursing. "I prayed as he hit me, but the prayers won't do any good because after every line of prayer, I cursed the bastard to hell. My thoughts were to heck with that forgiveness shit, I'll choke that bastard with his own balls when the war ends...and that was a promise." The other POWs were not permitted to help Andrew until the Kid left the hut. They carried him to his cot and the boys covered for him at work the next day. Andrew was beaten so badly he couldn't get out of bed for a few days.

On December 14, Andrew wrote that Raymond Splude had died at 1700 hrs. "He was in the hospital for more than fifty days. I didn't see him since the middle of last month when he was shifted down to isolation." Ray was buried on the fifteenth. The pallbearers were Corporal Harold Nicholson, Peter Burns, Wardie Hamilton, Bernard Castongay, and Andrew. Lieutenant John McGreevy commanded the detachment and Captain Deloreay officiated at the funeral at Sham Shui Po Roman Catholic Church. He was buried at Argyle Cemetery next to Bob Barclay's remains. "George Raymond Splude hailed from Jacquet River, NB. He was a very good fellow," Andrew concluded.

Once again the next paragraph in Andrew's diary was completely blacked out beyond interpretation. Andrew said it detailed the murder of a Chinese worker. "I'll never forget what I witnessed that day. A coolie walked across the road to the gate. The Jap guard hit him with a long staff. He kept beating him long after the coolie fell. I saw the blood fly from his head. Poor bastard! After witnessing that I felt like a piece of me was gone forever. I hoped I didn't grow callous to it all. I wrote about the coolie in my diary but I knew I had to black it out, or risk losing it again. Besides, if the Kamloops Kid read it, he would beat the shit out of me."

The Kid slapped the POWs around all the time. The boys called him "Slap Happy." Andrew called him a bastard. "It was very humiliating to get a hard slap in the face when I couldn't slap back. I couldn't imagine anyone, back home, slapping me and me not punching back. I was only small, but the few that did try to pick on me soon found out I'd hit back." Andrew would tighten his bony fist to demonstrate his ability.

On the eighteenth, Andrew had to work without boots since he had loaned his out for food and cigarettes. He also received a letter from Paul Dallain who was doing very well with his weight climbing to eighty-two pounds, up from seventy-eight.

Rumours spread about another Red Cross parcel getting to the camp. Andrew said that Red Cross parcels were the lifeblood of the POWs. They lived for the parcels and some may have died without them.

On the twenty-first, Andrew wrote, "there was a big inspection by a Japanese general and some Red Cross representatives."

> The guards made us drink a gallon of water before the inspection. We believed that tactic was intended to make us look fatter. The Red Cross visitors were not allowed any closer than 100 feet from us. Many of the boys were whooping across the compound trying to get the Red Cross people to contact their folks at home. The Japanese were pissed. Before the inspection, they ordered *shizuka na koto*, which means silence. They didn't have the balls to beat us in front of the inspectors, but we knew we'd catch hell when they were gone.

On the twenty-third Andrew and company were told that the Canadian Government had sent them ¥10 for Christmas. "Not much, but at least we could buy food from the guards. I bought a pound of sugar," he said. On the twenty-fourth they received another Red Cross package. "Unknown to us, it would be the last package for a very long time," Andrew recalled. "The package landed just in time for Christmas. It sure made the boys happy, and we appreciated it very much. I got a package of biscuits and candy for Xmas. I traded it with the Japs."

On December 25, Andrew wrote that he received communion at midnight mass where there was a very large crowd in attendance. They had a great Christmas dinner consisting of Red Cross margarine and one can of meat and vegetables. "I got a gift from Captain William Frank Clarke, stockings, matches, 5 candy and 1 yen. It sure was appreciated." After dinner Andrew filled his pipe with cigarette butts and enjoyed a smoke while listening to his bunkmates tell stories of Christmas at home. Andrew chimed in with a Christmas story from his youth.

> Pop had been laid off from the railroad company and Mom's teaching contract was not renewed. We knew there was no money for Christmas, or for gifts. We were certain that it would be a very poor Christmas. My brothers and I sang in the midnight mass Christmas choir, so at least we had that, and a possible treat from the priest, if we were good.
>
> A few days before Christmas, my older brother Leo and I were rummaging through the attic in our old house. Leo picked up a cloth that covered something on a side table. There sat five hand-whittled whistles, Christmas gifts my father had made for us. Our family had no money, but it didn't matter that Christmas morning. The joyous sound of whistles filled our house, some candy from the priest and meat boiling in the pot made it one of the best Christmas Days ever.
>
> We didn't have much, and in retrospect, that Christmas was one of the best I ever had. I wish I could go back to those days right now.

The next day Andrew wrote that he had the opportunity to buy twenty-three packs of Royal Leaf cigarettes. He used his Red Cross money to make the purchase and he planned to trade them with the Japanese for food. He also ordered a bottle of whisky from a civilian guard named Gigno for ¥2.50. The next day the guard brought a bottle of B&B whisky in. Andrew wondered where that guard had found a bottle of English whisky. He said they each had a small swallow and then passed it around to the rest of the twenty or so fellows in his shack.

At the end of the month, Andrew wrote, they had another big inspection with approximately twenty big-shot Japanese, among them several generals. Something was up. Andrew suspected they would be transferred to Japan, perhaps to build an airport. The major inspection also fuelled rumours that repatriation was being considered, but Andrew had his doubts.

By Christmas 1942, after a year of slave labour in Hong Kong, the airport landing strip was looking good. Andrew said he thought the POWs would get a break. As they entered January 1943 they had little work to do and they were fed much better. Andrew assumed the Japanese were fattening the POWs for a trip to Japan. "I heard the last hell ship to Japan got torpedoed by the Americans. Some guys from down home were on that ship. I hoped that they were okay," Andrew wrote.

On New Year's Day 1943, Andrew wrote, "Started another year as a prisoner of war of Nippon, I hoped that it would be our last New Year's as prisoners of war. My wish for 1943 was that we'd be treated a lot better than the last year. If they gave us more to eat we might have a chance to live. In nineteen forty three I hope we're free." Andrew also wrote that he ate the largest meal since he had become a POW. For New Year's Day dinner he had meat and vegetables, greens, and pudding with sauce. After dinner he lay back and had a peaceful smoke of a pipe full of butts or, as the POWs called them, snipes.

Andrew said years later that while he was a POW he had the same reoccurring dream that was always about him at home. Mostly, he said, he dreamt about eating huge meals at his mother's table with his family. The worst part about the dream was waking up to hunger, Andrew would say as he involuntarily rubbed his stomach at the memory.

Andrew pointed out a note in the margin in the upper corner of the diary page, written in early January about the same time: "O'Leary said there'll be no more fighting between the British and her enemies, by December /43 the war will be over." Andrew wrote that he bet $25 with O'Leary that the war would not be over by December 1943. After reading that section, Andrew would say that he won the bet but wished he had lost it.

Andrew's diary continued to highlight the details of his daily activities. He recorded that he got ¥2 from Captain Clark. He also bought a bottle of shampoo from Kiamé, another Japanese guard, which he shared with five of his mates. He also bought three packages of cigarettes. The cigarettes were dry and tasted bad, but they had a good kick. They were so strong he could only smoke a few per day. On January 7, Andrew wrote that the canteen supplies were in. Using the remainder of his Christmas funds he bought one pair of sunglasses and two cans of Tiger Balm, an ointment used to relieve aches and pains. That date was a big day for the Russians and Poles, as it was their Christmas. The next Sunday Andrew attended church where he sent a letter home to his family. After mass he bought a can of candied ginger for ¥2.50, which he traded for a meat pie.

By then, many rumours were circulating about where the Canadians might be going. At 1130 hours on January 10, the POWs were called to muster stations on the double where they stayed until 1930 hours. The Japanese were selecting category A-1 men, which Andrew assumed was for a draft to Nippon. "Six hundred of us Canucks were picked for the draft. Where would we go to next? We didn't know. Many of the boys were nervous about it, because they knew what happened to the POWs in the last draft from there. The old hell ship was torpedoed on route to Nippon most of the men were lost at sea. I took the bad news the same as if I was playing cards and got a poor hand. Hopefully I would live to tell about it." In *The Battle for Hong Kong 1941-1945: Hostage to Fortune*, Oliver Lindsay writes that "A further 2,000 POWs including 1,184 Canadians were sent from Hong Kong to Japan."

For the next week the POWs who were chosen for the draft were inoculated for dysentery and cholera. They were swabbed several times for diphtheria and had several stool tests. Their skin was also inspected for disease or parasites. The men in the draft were asked by the Canadian command to write a letter to be sent home if they died. The letters would only be sent if the POW's death was confirmed, otherwise it would not be mailed. The inoculations were repeated several days later as part of the medical protocol. The stool test, swabs, and skin inspections were also repeated. On several days the POWs were ordered to stand to all day and be ready to move off.

Once again, rumours spread about where they would be sent. Andrew thought it might be Formosa or Nippon. He worried that his parents would not know where he was and assumed that he would not be able to write to them for a long time. So Andrew gave his friend Matias his shoes and ¥1 as payment to write a letter home for him as soon as Matias knew where they were sending Andrew. Matias was soldier with the Hong Kong Defense Corp during the battle and was not drafted with Andrew to go to Japan. On January 18, Andrew wrote in his diary that they were on stand-to ready to move off from 0945 until 1500 hours.

Andrew also noted that "Fidele Legacy was in very bad shape. He came out of Diphtheria hospital yesterday. He was turned down for draft to Nippon." Andrew recalled that Fidele was still in quarantine on departure day, so he took a long staff and pole-vaulted over the fence separating the camp from the quarantine site. The Japanese would shoot him if he was caught but he figured, the hell with it, Fidele needed him. Fidele's face was sunken in, his eyes were black and his voice was low and weak. His thin frame was half the size it had been the previous year. Andrew hoped he would recover. He gave Fidele ¥2, his new pair of sunglasses, and two packages of cigarettes so he could trade them after Andrew was shipped out.

To cheer him up Andrew talked about some of their antics in the army during better times. Andrew remembered their conversation.

"Remember the day we joined?"
"Yeah, Andrew, you shouldn't have got reweighed."
"But look at all the fun we would have missed," I joked.
Fidele smiled and said it wasn't worth it.

"Mercifully, I didn't know that was the last time I would see poor Fidele," Andrew said. "God bless him, he remained forever at stand-to in Hong Kong."

Chapter Seven

Hell Ships to Japan
and Camp D Yokohama

Translating with the use of his Japanese dictionary for a year helped Andrew to become familiar with the language. He often eavesdropped on the Japanese guards' conversations. For the first two weeks of 1943 the guards were obsessed with the impending shift of the POWs away from Hong Kong. For the most part the guards did not want to go back to Japan. Apparently the army was much stricter there.

On January 18, the 662 Canadians who were previously drafted marched to Kowloon harbour where the Japanese eventually packed them into a hell ship and the next morning they left. Many of Andrew's friends from home boarded the ship with him. Only the sick and wounded stayed in Hong Kong. The name "hell ships" came from the vessels where the fellows were packed in the storage areas with no open air. During the Second World War many POWs of Japan died on these ships from the heat and horrible conditions.

Andrew wrote that they slept on the cement dock at Kowloon dock until they were put on stand-to at 0500 hours and the POWs boarded the ship *Tatsuta Maru* at 0900 hours. Andrew shared a cabin with a number of other POWs. He also received ¥10 from the Red Cross before boarding. Many of the old barges had bulk storage holds where POWs were loaded and the hatches were shut above them. Andrew was lucky because he was one of twelve men crammed into a two-person cabin on the ship. They were packed like sardines and Andrew felt smothered, so he pushed his way to the side where he got a good seat on the top bunk; there, he could hang on to the open porthole and get some fresh air. He and Abe Driscoll, who was from Andrew's hometown, clung to that spot for the duration of the journey.

On January 20, Andrew reported, the China Sea was very choppy. They experienced a terrible rain storm with lightning striking all around them, blazing the horizon with a frightening orange glow. They were cold all night but the next day was sweltering. Most of the time on board, they were uncomfortable. "At least I had open air," Andrew said. "The poor bastards in the hold suffered unbearable heat in the day, and froze at night." Quite a few men were seasick, but Andrew felt fine.

Fortunately, Andrew's journey was short. On January 22, they docked at Nagasaki, Japan. "We were on stand-to for the disembarkation from the ship at 0500 hours, but only got off the ship 10 hours later at 1500 hours at a big Japanese city that I never heard of before called Naggasaccy. By 2300 hours we boarded a very modern but crowded train."

The passenger train was cramped, with many people in the aisles and baggage areas. Once again, Andrew was lucky; the Hong Kong Volunteers and some of the Chinese were packed into freight cars connected to the rear of the train. However, Joe Landry and Andrew shared a bench seat with three other POWs. By January 23, Andrew recorded, they were at Okayama where meals were put on the train. "One box of cooked rice or barley & one box of fish, carrots, potatoes, salad, kelp dolce and maggots one & a half inches long. I was hungry, the grub was good."

After spending a year starving in Hong Kong, most of the POWs considered maggots protein and protein was good, although Andrew preferred to eat them in the dark.

They felt a sense of grave anticipation on the train, Andrew wrote. "Many of the fellows from Jacquet River had disembarked at various stations. Arnold Courier (Carrier), Ernest Meade, and Ernest Miller left us at Kawasaki where they were forced to work for the Omine Coal mines. They were selected by guards as the train stopped. I and many of the others were anxious about what fate awaited us. We talked about the guards stealing our food when we were building the airport in Hong Kong. I assumed that was why they fed us so well before we departed. Perhaps that explained the Hong Kong guard's reluctance to be shipped with us to Nippon."

Andrew also assumed the Japanese gave them new clothing as they departed to make it look like they'd been treated better than they really were. As for the inoculations, Andrew presumed that the Japanese didn't want the POWs to start an outbreak on their island. Obviously, the many POW deaths from communal diseases like dysentery, cholera, and diphtheria were a concern for Japan.

On Sunday, January 24, Andrew wrote about arriving at their new POW camp. "We arrived at Yokohama at 0645 hours and left at 0710 hours on an electric train. We then marched about 3 miles to our new camp. At first glance it looked like a real POW camp. It looked like it was fixed up according to Red Cross plans, including a swimming pool. The hut I was in held over two hundred men. We were each issued 5 bamboo blankets as soon as we got in camp. Some of the other POWs disembarked earlier at Osaka on the 23rd."

It didn't take long before Andrew figured out that the camp was designed just for show. In reality, the camp was a hellhole. The swimming pool was a communal bath that smelled like sewage, the buildings were infested with rats, lice, and bed bugs, there were not enough blankets to keep them warm at night, and there was no source of heat in the buildings. As he learned, Japan in the winter was much colder than Hong Kong.

On his second day in Camp D Yokohama, Andrew wrote, reveille was at 0600. It was so cold the water taps were frozen. That was the first ice he had seen since he left home in 1941. There was no stove or heat source in his hut and, although he had several blankets, he hadn't been able to warm up during the night. Andrew and the other POWs were assigned to work at the Nippon Steel Tube-Tsurumi Shipyards. Work parties were usually small groups of prisoners, mixed with Japanese civilian workers and a boss. Andrew worked twelve-hour days drilling sheets of steel at the dock. He often worked high up on bamboo scaffolds that wrapped around a ship like a veil. Each rickety scaffold section was about three metres high; four sections were approximately twelve metres high. Some scaffolds stretched over twenty-four metres in the air and were secured tenuously to parts of the ship. The POW workers were not equipped with proper clothing, tools, or safety gear. Andrew wrote that he "drilled upon the outside of a

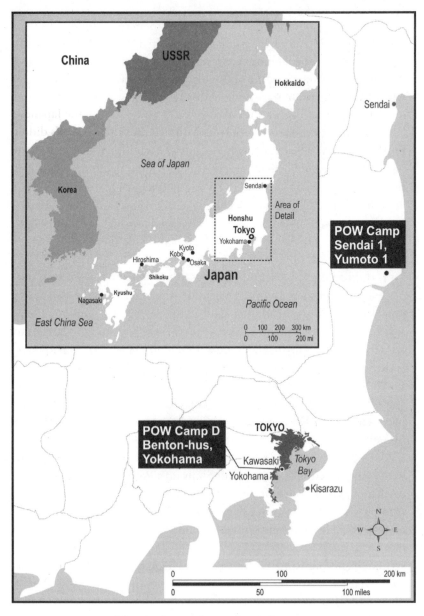

Map of prisoner of war camps in Japan. MB

ship today, drilling overhead. The drill kicked back and broke my thumb. It nearly knocked me off the scaffolding. I saw a coolie go to Davy Jones off the derrick sling, he plunged about 80 feet to his death." Nor were they were fed adequately. Fortunately, barley was plentiful, which was a nice change from the usual rice.

In the camp and at work the POWs had to take orders in the Japanese language. Andrew had few problems with that, but many POWs didn't understand the commands, so the Japanese would strike and beat them until they conformed. Since the Japanese at the shipyard didn't speak English, Andrew and many other POWs took full advantage of their language barrier. In the morning, while marching to work, they were forced to bow and pray to what they saw as a pagan god in a grotto next to their path. A number of men from Andrew's hometown entertained themselves by tricking the Japanese into thinking that they were praying. "With all the piety and reverence we could muster up we'd chant [insults]," Andrew said. "We all tried to outdo each other. The hardest part was not laughing at some of the outrageous vulgarities. The Jap guards were all smiles when they thought the boys were praying to their pagan god. Until one day we got a bad beating. Apparently, the new interpreter told the Japs what we were up to. Some people said he was the Kamloops Kid, but I knew the difference and I was glad it was not him."

February 1 was Andrew's birthday. He thought of his mother making a fuss about the date; she would surely have baked a cake for the occasion. "I had barley and soup instead in a place I didn't want to be," he would say.

The first week of February was all work with no time off, drilling and more drilling until his arms felt like they were dead. His broken thumb was taped tight to his index finger, making it hard to hold onto the drill. He hadn't had time to wash his clothes. "Lousy again and no wonder," he wrote. "I worked in the rain and snow drilling on the outside of the ship. I was four scaffolds up, almost 40 feet. I was soaked to skin and very cold by the end of the shift. I got a box of matches from a Nip worker, but it was too wet to light a fire. Back at the camp I froze all night again. I'd probably catch a cold or worse," he wrote. By the end of that week he was feverish and felt very fatigued. He was drilling on the fifth scaffolding height, and he almost fainted with flu-like symptoms so he had to go see a Japanese medic. He gave Andrew a pill and told him to go back to work. "I shan't forget that morning," Andrew recorded. "It had rained like hell, there was from two to four inches of water across the streets and we had to walk to the dock in it. My sneakers and clothes were soaked. I didn't get a chance to change them all day. I won't be surprised if I get rheumatism or sciatica. That was the second day in two weeks where I was wet all day. We finally got a stove going that night. It was only the size of a ten pound shortening can and it gave off very little heat."

The following week was much the same. It was very cold working on the boat all week. Andrew witnessed a "ram pike" being turned over to the Japanese navy. (This might be code for a submarine.) They also had three little stoves in their hut by then.

Andrew had no fear of heights, but when the wind blew at eight scaffolds (almost twenty-five metres) up, the rickety scaffolds swayed and made cracking noises, which was unnerving. One day, he heard a crash and several men screamed. As he turned he saw an adjacent scaffold collapse. In a matter of seconds, four Chinese workers crashed onto the dock below.

Andrew wrote, "After working 11 day straight we POWs got a day off. The Japs held a kit and diary inspection. I got in trouble because I had a Japanese propaganda leaflet which I drew filthy things on. They also asked about the colored cloth that I had rolled up in my kitbag. I told them it was bandage cloth. I was happy the guard didn't unravel it. Truth be told, it was the Union Jack that I saved when we were captured at Stanley Fort. Bliss Cole and I had meat and potatoes for dinner. We sure needed a good meal. We pitched in and bought the stuff from a Japanese worker at the dock. I also received three tangerines and 15 yen from the camp officer." Andrew also recorded that he got a "black bald haircut," meaning a shaved head. It was the only way to keep the lice under control without paraffin oil. Some of the POWs got caught by the guards trading on the ship. They were slapped severely, he wrote.

On Valentine's Day, Andrew woke up "as blind as a bat," he wrote. He managed to walk to the docks where a site nurse fixed his eyes by removing iron filings that had flown from the drill bits. Andrew said the

POWs didn't have safety glasses, so when he drilled overhead the filings fell into his eyes. It was very painful and annoying.

In mid-February Andrew got paid a small amount of cash, ¥2. However, the money didn't come from the Japanese; the POWs were paid by Captain W.F. Clark, Jr. Andrew figured it was Red Cross money distributed by the camp command.

One day, he wrote, he was on a work party and saw a fellow POW killed by a drill bit through his head. They were working over twenty-five metres up when the drill kicked back and the bit broke, shooting back and killing the operator. That night he said he was homesick. He bought a cookie and five cigarettes for ¥15. For the balance of the week, he said, they worked hard and launched a ship on the weekend.

The ship was built for the Japanese merchant marine as a cargo transport and was constructed by Nippon Steel Tube-Tsurumi Shipyards with the help of POW slave labour. Andrew recalled their acts of resistance at some length.

> Throughout our stay at the shipyard we figured out how to keep fighting for home. We did what we could to slow or stop production such as drilling the steel plates in the wrong place or cutting the steel too short. Other times we messed with the finished product. After drilling and riveting steel plates to the ship, a Japanese inspector usually came around and tapped each rivet to see if it was solid. After the inspection some of the boys from down home would grind the back of the rivets, just leaving enough to hold the steel in place. It was rumoured that when these ships went out to sea they sank as the waves work the rivets loose. We become very good at exacting that bit of revenge...so good that by the time the fourth ship was launched it sank shortly thereafter in the middle of Tokyo Bay. Unfortunately, the Japanese suspected sabotage and tried to beat a confession out of us. No one talked. If we admitted anything we'd all be killed. I figured it was better to put up with the beating than to die.

For our joint punishment, they shipped us off to the coal mines where we really suffered.

George S. MacDonell, another Royal Rifles soldier, confirmed in his autobiography, *One Soldier's Story*, that the Canadians actively practised sabotage in the shipyards. He wrote that he was too sick to perform hard labour so the Japanese had him packing grease in bearings. "From time to time, my unsuspecting foreman assigned me the easy job of filling the grease reservoirs over the ships' engine bearings. Despite the misery and growing despair of our situation, I never missed an opportunity, when undetected, to first fill the grease caps with iron filings before filling the rest of the cap with thick grease. Once at sea, the iron filings would burn out the bearings."

On February 24, Andrew was working on the *Hidaka Maru*, which was docked to the wharf. It was having leaking issues after it was launched, Andrew said with a sheepish smile. "The Americans torpedoed it the next year," he said with a certain pleasure. According to the website http://wrecksite.eu/wreck.aspx?136541, "On 20th January 1944, US submarine USS *Batfish* (SS-310) attacked a Japanese convoy off southern Honshu and torpedoed the Japanese transport *Hidaka Maru*, south of Shiono Misaki."

The twenty-sixth was a busman's holiday, Andrew wrote. They were on stand-to all day for medicals. He got four needles and was told by the nurse that the needles were very good for him. He also noted, "We buy biscuits and other food from the crew and guards with our meagre pay. We also have our own canteen, but the officers usually get first choice. Some of the fellows were pissed because the officers always got first crack at the canteen supplies. I was glad that they left something for us. I bought 14 biscuits for 15 sen. They were very fresh and good."

On the last day of February, reveille was at 0530 hours. Andrew went for another medical before catching up to his work party. He said he got a kick in the backside from a Japanese worker for operating the drill recklessly. He drilled through the steel plates and into the deck three times that morning. And not always on purpose, he would say with a laugh. "If I didn't pay attention I'd drill right through the plates. It was hard to focus when hunger was my main preoccupation and my thumb was useless."

At the beginning of March, the weather was a little better. Andrew lifted and assembled steel most of the first week. The fourth was a day off and he got 35 sen, which he used to buy ten cigarettes and some candy.

"On March 4," he said, "I wrote a letter home. I didn't know if it would ever get there. I fantasized about the route my letter would take across the Pacific and across Canada to home. I wished I could crawl into the envelope and go home with the letter. Silly, I knew, to think such thoughts, but that was how I survived."

The end of that week brought an inspection by a very high-ranking Japanese officer. He was in charge of all the POWs, according to the guards. He said a few words to the effect that the POWs were Nippon POWs and Nippon was at war with our countries and the world, and would be until she accomplished what she set out to do, namely the destruction of our countries. Until then, the officer said that the POWs would be treated humanely. He concluded by asking the POWs to look after each other. "I would have liked to believe him, but I knew as soon as he took a powder, we'd be back to the same old shit with the Nip guards. And right I was, that night it was rice only again for supper."

The next week Andrew and his work party were transferred to work on the *Ginga Maru*. He bought ten cigarettes and four bananas. "That was the first banana I had since we were captured," Andrew said. "I shared it with Charlie Dellain. He made monkey noises as he ate the fruit. Charlie was always good for a laugh. We licked the peelings clean."

On the tenth Andrew wrote that his name was taken by the dock police when he was caught with his money purse out in the bow of the *Hidaka Maru*. He said he thanked his boss, Akiba, for saving him from getting a beating. Akiba was a decent Japanese civilian boss. He told the dock police that he had asked Andrew to show him what he had in his purse, which was a lie. Andrew was actually paying Akiba for food. The ship sailed off that night.

Tokyo was bombed for the first time since they got there, Andrew wrote in his diary. The next day Andrew and crew were assigned to a new ship under construction. "The boss, Akiba, was tops. He let me hide down in the hold all afternoon for forty winks," Andrew wrote. He said later, "I hoped we'd get to keep Akiba. There wasn't much to do on a new ship for us. Akiba hid and told us to do the same. I wrapped up in a jute sack and had a great sleep. I dreamt I was home. I loved dreaming about home, it was almost worth the disappointment of reality after awakening."

Soon Andrew was back working on the frame and superstructure of the new ship. One day he saw a freighter come into port with great damage to the front of its superstructure. It looked like it had collided with another ship. Another day he had a feast on the dock when they found some potatoes at work and baked them in the charcoal used to heat the rivets.

On the sixteenth he wrote that he got steel in his left eye again. The next day, St. Patrick's Day, Andrew wrote, "I hope to be home next St. Patrick's. I reported the steel in my eye and was taken to M.J. [a site medic] then to the hospital. The doctor took out the steel. It was very painful. I think he enjoyed my discomfort."

St. Patrick's Day was always a special day at Andrew's home. His family would have a few drinks and sing some old Irish songs as well as eat a large boiled dinner. In the POW camp, as he thought of being home for the occasion, he said he could almost taste the cabbage, potatoes, turnips, and salt pork. "I ate a bowl of rice that night and imagined it was filled with Mom's boiled diner. Have I mentioned yet that I hated rice?" he would ask satirically.

On March 19, he wrote that he saw a POW killed at the dock and that a bad guard nicknamed Horseface had *put the brogues* to Morrison. Andrew tried to confuse the Japanese who read his diary by using words and sayings from home, such as "brogues" to mean kicking. It worked when the Japanese read his writing, but there was no fooling the Japanese turncoats from Canada or others who had studied in English countries before the war.

From March 20 to mid-April, Andrew's diaries recorded the hard labour, lack of food, and, in general, harsh circumstances the POWs endured. One entry said, "I saw a POW fall from the scaffolding today. He died on impact with the water, thus he enters Davy Jones' Locker. I worked all day in heavy rain and cold. No smokes."

On April 20 he wrote that Akiba was accused by Horseface of not working the POWs hard enough. "Joe Landry and I made our way over to the bow of the ship where they were arguing. We pretended we were afraid of Akiba. Joe begged Akiba not to beat us anymore. Joe had cut his hand earlier and told Horseface that Akiba was working him to the bone. He flashed his cut hand as proof to Horseface. All of it was a charade. Akiba was the best boss we ever had. He never hit us. Horseface must have bought the ruse because he left and didn't report Akiba." At the end of the war, Andrew said, he and Joe visited Akiba at his home and had dinner with his family before returning to Canada.

On Good Friday, they had whale blubber for supper. "It was delicious," Andrew wrote. "I wondered if I would eat whale blubber at home. Probably not! It was very viscous and had a 10W30 motor oil flavour to it. Being malnourished as I was, it sure did taste good. I wished I had more." They had April 25, Easter Sunday, off. To most Japanese it was the same as any other Sunday, Andrew would say. "We had a quiet observation with a lay minister leading our service."

One night they had bamboo shoots cooked in water with salt. They tasted much better than rice, Andrew said. The texture and flavour reminded him of home. "It tasted like the soft, chewable end of a ripe straw of hay."

On the Emperor's birthday, April 29, the POWs got a few hours off work. "We got three hours off as a holiday to observe the emperor's birthday. I wished him, for his birthday, a quick and timely death. I considered him the cause of the war and our misery. I tried not to hate the ordinary people of Nippon, but I despised their government and their war machine, including their cruel guards. I bought an old apple that day. The skin was wrinkled like an old man's face, but it sure tasted like home. I planted ten apple trees on Dr. Smith's property in 1933; Macintosh, Courtland, and a few other types. I picked the first crop the year before I joined the army."

On May 4, Andrew said, the Japanese read his diary and censored the parts they didn't like. They searched all of the POWs' belongings. The

POWs knew that when the Japanese found cigarettes, they often took them (and usually sold them back to the POWs), so they had to hide them carefully.

A few days later they had another three-hour holiday. Andrew didn't know why. He said he found a sewing needle that day. He unravelled the thread from an old stocking and used it to sew up his pants and shirt. The fellows in his hut each did the same with their rags, Andrew said.

"On May 27 I sent a card to Bud [his younger brother], [what] a coincidence that on the following night May 28 I got my first word from Canada since I left in '41: a letter from Bud written on November 13, 1942. I was delighted to hear that all was okay at home."

> May 26, 1943
> Dear Buddy:
>
> I am in the best of health, hope you are all the same.
> Give my best wishes to all my friends. I suppose Roge is still
> at home, the best place for him.
> Best regards to ma, pa, brothers and Rita.
>
> Ando

Andrew had suspected that the Japanese were sitting on the POWs' letters. The date on Bud's letter confirmed his contention, but he admitted that it was nice to hear from home. "I didn't want my family worried about me so I always proclaimed to be in the best of health," Andrew would say. "Truth be known, I was very sick. Most days I couldn't even write in my diary; I was too exhausted after work...I just had to sleep, but many times hunger prevented a good sleep." On June 16, he wrote, "I got my first full day off work since I started here. I was very sick, my malaria was back again. The next day I was sent out to work again. I walked through a foot of rain on some streets. It was pouring. I had no rain-cape. I had a fever as bad as ever for a week and half, I won't forget it. JAF"

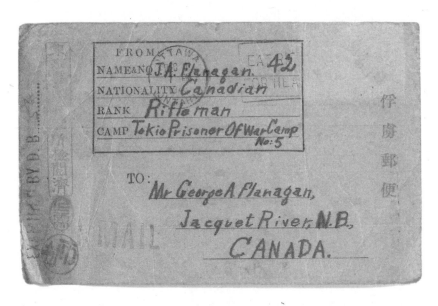

FROM OTTAWA
NAME & NO. *J.A. Flanagan* 42
NATIONALITY *Canadian*
RANK *Rifleman*
CAMP *Tokio Prisoner Of War Camp*
No: 5

TO: *Mr George A Flanagan,*
    Jacquet River, N.B.,
    CANADA.

DATE *May 26, 1943.*

Dear Buddy,
        I am in the best
of health, hope you are all the same.
Give my best wishes to all my
friends, I suppose Roge is still at home
the best place for him.
        Best regards to ma and pa, brothers
and Rita.
        Ando

Card sent by Andrew to his brother Bud on May 26, 1943. AFC

Andrew heard many rumours about the Pope sending money through the Red Cross to the Japanese to buy the POWs new boots. The Red Cross had previously reported that most POWs were in need of foot rigging. The Japanese gave the POWs each a pair of paper boots and the rain turned them into porridge on contact. "I guess the Japs gave the Pope's boots to their soldiers," Andrew surmised.

"On July 1st at 1400 hours a severe earthquake struck the shipyard," Andrew wrote. "Joe Frenette, Akiba & I were plating on the bow and could not get off the ship. The Japs deserted the ship." In the middle of July, Andrew also wrote that he had diarrhea non-stop for three days. His boss let him off easy at work because of his condition. Akiba, he wrote, was still a good boss. "He traded plenty with us knowing that if he got caught he would be in trouble too."

Andrew wrote a letter to his sister Rita on July 26.

Dear Rita

I am glad to have this opportunity to write to you and let you know I am in good health. I have received two letters so far, one from Doctor Smith, the other from Bud, got them the latter part of May, up to the time the letters were sent everyone was well. I hope they have all continued being in good health.

I imagine you have graduated by now also Bud. Did you get the silk outfit of clothes I sent to you from China? Do you get home often, and how do you find mother and Dad, is Roge still home?

As my space is about taken up I shall wind up this letter. I hope that in the very near future we shall get together again.

Love Ando

"I really didn't want to stop writing to her," Andrew explained while reading his diaries. "I had a strange connection with home when I wrote to anyone. I felt that an extension of me went with the letter back home.

I missed my family. I missed my younger siblings most because I missed seeing them become adults. I missed so much at home it made me feel anxious. Some days I just wanted to run home."

On August 1, the shipyard company took over the camp and the care of the POWs, including their food. At that time, Andrew thought the company would be worse than the Japanese army. On August 6, another earthquake struck, Andrew recorded. At the end of August Andrew wrote that the diarrhea he'd had last month had come back and would not stop.

Andrew's family received more news about him. On September 3, they received correspondence from Colonel F.W. Clarke, Sr. at the Department of National Defence with an update and instructions for future correspondence:

> I am now able to inform you that the diplomatic exchange vessel "GRIPSHOLM" sailed on 2nd September, 1943, carrying foodstuffs and medical supplies for the Far East.
>
> Since then, notice has been received from the Japanese Government that in the future letters to prisoners of war in their hands must not contain more than 24 words (exclusive of address). It is understood that this limit will apply only to mail written after the present date and will not affect letters already sent on the GRIPSHOLM.

On September 9, Andrew's folks received their first letter from him since he became a POW. It was dated March 4, 1943. In the Department of National Defence files they quoted part of that letter:

CASUALTIES

Wrote to mother: "I am in the best of Health. Robert Barclay is dead."
Correspondence "Wrote care of Red Cross Geneva, to address on letter."

Back in Japan things didn't get better when the Nippon Kokan shipyard company took over. The Japanese guards were still in control of the POWs and the company only provided rations, which decreased as the war dragged on, Andrew wrote. Japan was running out of food and resources. They could hardly feed their own troops, let alone their population. POWs were the least of their concern as food got more scarce. "I continued to write in my diary when my health permitted, albeit more sparingly. I was running out of paper and lead was harder to get. Mostly I wrote with a piece of lead less than an inch long. I recorded all mistreatments, beatings, and degradation between September 1943 and April 1945 when we were shifted from the shipyards to Sendai Coal Mine.

"Starvation and disease were taking their toll on me," he continued. "I was losing weight steadily; by the end of 1943 I weighed 85 pounds. By the end of 1944 I weighed much less. Most of the boys in our camp were suffering the same fate. Joe Landry and the other young soldiers were growing up to be fine young men. In an ironic twist of fate, the young men were taking care of me when I couldn't. Poor young fellows, they should have been working at home or studying, not in a POW camp starving to death."

On October 1, the Japanese gave each POW a number. No man was allowed to eat until he knew his number in Japanese. If a man couldn't pronounce it right, he was beaten and sent away from the food area.

Very few fellows in the camp knew their numbers in Japanese. My number was *shi-ju-ni*, [She-Jew-Knee, spelled phonetically, or forty-two]. I was hungry but before I ate that day I walked around to all the men in my shack with my dictionary and helped them figure out how to pronounce their number in Japanese. It was late before I got to eat. Our POW numbers were sequential beginning at one. We usually sounded off three times a day. We all got to know how to count in Japanese by listening to the roll call; one, two, three, four, five, six, seven, eight, nine, ten etc. [*ici, ni, san, shi, go, roku, shichi, hachi, ku, ju.*] If a POW forgot how to pronounce his number, he was dealt with severely by the Japs.

At the shipyards, Andrew recalled, a Japanese civilian named Yuki was assigned to work with him, and he acted like he was Andrew's boss.

The lazy little bastard always tried to get me to do his work. On October 6, 1943, we were drilling on a ship in dry dock. "Andrew, you drill," Yuki said to me in Nip. I was mostly fluent in Nip by then. "The hell with you, I drilled all day. It's your turn," I answered in Nip. He threw the drill at me, I ducked. The drill hit the bamboo scaffolding and pulled the planks out from under my feet. I remember seeing everything in slow motion. I was falling to the deck below. There was a stack of steel plates slightly to my left and an open hatch slightly to my right. I fell the twenty or so feet in a split second. I landed squarely on my elbow between the steel and the hatch. Yuki told Horseface, our Japanese boss, that it was my fault. I got a beating, and so did Yuki, which gladdened my heart. Watching one Nip beat another cheered me up. Horseface hit me hard, but he hit Yuki harder. Ha! My elbow was broken. The medic wrapped my arm to my chest, rendering it immobile. I got two days off work. Back at work, my arm was useless. It just hung around for the next few months. It only hurt when I tried to move it.

By the end of November, Andrew's arm was healed, but then he had another accident at work when he was struck by falling steel and knocked off the scaffold. Fortunately, he didn't reinjure his elbow, but he did hurt his head. The doctor's report read:

Andrew Flanagan Contusion Skull
POW CAMP MEDICAL RECORD
Dec. 4 No complications still slight giddiness with rapid movement. Discharged to hut.
Initialled R

All Canada joins
in
Warmest Christmas Greetings
and good wishes to you

W.L. Mackenzie King

1943   Prime Minister

Christmas greeting from Canadian Prime Minster W.L. Mackenzie King. AFC

On December 5 Andrew went back to work. On the twenty-third he recorded that the Canadian POWs received a postcard from the Prime Minister of Canada. It read:

> All Canada joins in Warmest Christmas Greetings and good wishes to you.
> [signed] W.L. Mackenzie King Prime Minister 1943

"Some of the boys use the card to roll cigarette butts," Andrew wrote. "I think perhaps they were Conservatives. I saved mine. I sure hoped to be home for next Christmas."

On the twenty-fifth Andrew wrote that it was a hungry Christmas. "I wondered what was happening at home. I knew mom was cooking a great feast; a goose Pop chose from his flock, potatoes, carrots and turnips from our garden, and fruitcake for dessert. I tried to imagine that I was home partaking in their joy. The boring taste of rice jolted me back to reality. I'd never eat rice again if I got out of that God awful place I promised myself."

The company did not provide enough food. A group of fellows killed a number of rats and roasted them for Christmas dinner. They said it tasted like chicken. Andrew said he wouldn't eat rats or snakes. The next day, Andrew was glad he hadn't eaten the rat. "The boys who ate Christmas dinner last night were shitting a blue streak. Something in the rat meat didn't agree with their system. I'd starve before I'd eat a rat," he would say. On January 1, 1944, Andrew wrote, "Another New Years as a POW, I hoped it would be my last. I feared it may be because I wouldn't survive another year. There was a lot less food this year. New Year's Mass was low key."

By mid-January, Andrew was lousy again. Working with the Japanese population, climbing scaffolds behind them, no wonder he was lousy, he would say. "Albert Murchie had some coal oil in his tool kit. I soaked my head with it. It killed the lice and nits, instantly. I hoped that no one would light a cigarette next to me. We often put a small amount of oil in the wash water to try to kill the bed bugs in our blankets and our clothing. It worked somewhat, but before too long we were re-infested."

In January Andrew wrote home:

Dear Mother and Father

It is a pleasure to be allowed to write again to let you know I am still in good health. I would like to be home for Easter, but I reckon [I'll] be lucky enough to be with you for Xmas; my thoughts are always with you and I hope everything is going well with you, and do not worry about me. I'll pull through all right. At Xmas we got half a Red Cross food parcel, expect a whole parcel soon.

Fred Elsliger today got a parcel from his mother. I got 3 letters from Dr. Smith; hope he is in good health; give him and my friends my best regards. One from Mrs. K. Doyle, Bud, and your letter with snap shots which were very good. I suppose Roge still has his horses well groomed. Bud is working now I presume, also Rita. I have not seen Fidele since I left China.

Joe Landry, Joe Frenette, and Fred Elsliger and other local boys send best wishes.

Ando

Andrew received a picture of his mother in a letter. He said he kept it in his breast pocket, close to his heart. When he got homesick he'd take it out and listen to his mother's encouragement in his head. "I heard the words she spoke years before when I was just a lad. 'Be strong, be brave, have no fear; you are not alone.'" "Don't worry Mom, I heard you," Andrew would tell her before slipping the snapshot back into his pocket. It sounded crazy, he'd say, but it helped him cope.

On February 24 Andrew received a parcel from home. "Nips rifled through it, God only knows what they stole. Mom was so smart, in the parcel, on top of the socks and underwear was a blank note book with a full pencil attached. How did she know?" Andrew wondered.

On March 4 Andrew wrote,

Yuki was as lazy as ever. We were perched about 60 feet up the ship, attaching accessories. He wanted me to tighten the bolts with his spanner. 'No Yuki, that's your job,' I said in Nip. He swung all he could and struck the back of my head with the wrench. I felt the warm blood running down my back. I turned fast to face him and hit him a pile-driver punch to the guts. It lifted both of his feet off the planks. He landed hard, doubled over. He dropped to the outside of the planks. I grabbed him by the scruff of his neck and held him until he revived.

Tokyo, No: 3, D Camp,
January 13, 1944.

Dear Mother, and Father   It is a
pleasure to be allowed to write again to
let you know I am still in good health.
I would like to be home for Easter, but I
reckon be lucky enough to be with you for
Xmas, my thoughts are always with you
and I hope everything is going well with you,
and do not worry about me, I'll pull through
all right. At Xmas we got half a Red Cross
Food parcel, expect a whole parcel soon.

First page of Andrew's letter to his parents written on January 13, 1945. AFC

"What's going on up there?" Horseface called from down below in Nip.

"Nothing," I replied, "Yuki slipped and I caught him."

"That's not true, Ando punched me," Yuki said spitefully.

"Come down here, both of you!" Horseface barked. "Come, we go see Tojo." He spit the words out.

Tojo was the nickname given to the Japanese supervisor because he looked like Prime Minister Hideki Tōjō. Both had given me many beatings since I came to the shipyards, but not that day. "Ha ha, that's funny," I said in Nip as we walked to the office. "Two Japanese get a beating but only one Canadian. Yuki gets a beating, Ando gets a beating and Horseface gets a beating." At the steps of the office I was tapped on the head by Horseface. He twirled his index finger in a circular motion, indicating we were turning around. No beating today.

The Japanese superiors, like Tojo, often beat the POWs, but they also beat the Japanese bosses and their co-workers to keep them in line. Horseface knew exactly what would happen to him and Yuki if he continued into the office.

In April of 1944, on another occasion, Andrew said, "I and another Canadian got a slapping from Horseface. A fellow POW working on rivets saw the whole affair. He called to us after Horseface left. 'Hey fellas, you want to get even with Horseface?' 'You know it!' we answered. 'Next time you see him walking this way, yell out *bull's eye*, and see some fun.'"

I worked drilling on high scaffolds that day. My friend who was also slapped was working on the scaffold next to me. We had a bird's eye view from forty feet up. The riveting crew was working right below me. The fellow we talked to was a heater. He heated the rivets red hot then pitched them with thongs to a catcher. The catcher placed the hot rivet into a drilled hole and the riveter hammered the rivet in place. I kept my eyes peeled all day. Finally, I saw Horseface heading toward our location. As he walked in front of the scaffold we both yelled, "Bull's eye!" The pitcher sent a rivet to the catcher, and the riveting crew worked on that one. He flung a second red hot rivet high over the catcher's head, past the base of my scaffold. I saw a puff of white smoke as it hit Horseface in the back of the head and trailed down his shirt. I almost fell off my perch laughing. Everyone quickly went back to work. Horseface yelled as he ripped off his clothes. He looked all around but there were too many workers on the site to identify the person responsible for his pain.

"That was one of my better days at the shipyards," Andrew chuckled.

Food and cigarettes were getting harder to come by. In the spring of 1944, rations were cut. Many of Andrew's friends died from disease, starvation, and exhaustion. He later revealed that he wondered if any of them would see Canada again.

"In May I sent a shortwave radio message for myself and a few other boys from down home. It took a bribe but it was worth the risk. Akiba told me that he heard names and hometowns of POWs on Japanese shortwave Radio Tokyo. So I figured out how to send a message. I had to follow the Nip outline, but I was sure the folks back home would read between the lines. I didn't mind saying some of it because I didn't want Mom to worry about me."

On May 16, the following message was broadcast as presented by Andrew on Tokyo Radio International:

To: Mrs. James Flanagan. It is a pleasure for me to be allowed to let you know that I am in good health and looking forward to the day when I shall be with you all once again. I received your parcel some time ago and several letters. Many of the boys from home have received a clothing parcel and letters. There are with me here from Jacquet River, who wish to be remembered to their relatives and friends, Alfred Elsliger, Abe

Driscoll, John Killoran, Albert Murchie, and Leo Pitre (Pete), Jean Lapointe, Joseph Landry from Charlo. Time is limited, so I will say goodbye and good luck. From Andrew Flanagan.

"The next day at work Akiba told me he heard my broadcast. I wondered if it would get picked up or sent home. It made me feel good to send it anyway. Many of the other boys are also sending shortwave messages."

All that summer and into the fall, letters from home told the boys in POW Camp D that their folks got cards from shortwave radio enthusiasts on the west coast of North America. The radio listeners recorded the broadcasts on cards by hand or some recorded them on cardboard disks. Most listed the names of the lads from home. Only the west coast could pick up the regular broadcast from Radio Tokyo. Andrew's mother received 100 cards and letters, ten on some days, from all over the west coast. Complete strangers wrote to her from California, Washington, Alaska, and Alberta. Empathy for a mother's worry motivated those wartime citizens. The letters quoted Andrew's broadcast, all saying basically the same thing.

Andrew's mother received an impressive official copy of a report from the United States Pacific Fleet, Air Force, Blimp Squadron thirty-one.

United States Pacific Fleet,
Air Force,
Blimp Squadron Thirty One

Mrs. J. Flanagan.
Jacquette River.,
New Brunswick, Canada.

Dear Mrs. Flanagan,
   Every night I listen to the prisoners of War from Tokyo, Japan, on short-wave radio here at this station.
   Tonight I heard the following message from your son

Andrew Flanagan, 28 yrs of age who was a rifle-man with the army in China.

"I am in good health, and do not worry too much as I will be alright. I receive your letters and parcels OK. He also sent his regards either to the following men or from them. It was noisy on the air and I did not hear which way he meant the regards, but their names were as follows, Alfred E ? ., Abe Driscoll, John Killeran, Elbert ? , Joseph Landrey. Located at Ontario. Good luck and God bless you all. Andrew."

Trusting that this letter will give you a little consolation in knowing that he is alive and well, and if I should happen to hear him on the air again, please rest assured that I will not hesitate to let you know at once.

Yours for a quicker victory.
Stephen G. Spicer S2/c U.S. Navy
P.S. Please advise me of receipt of this letter.

"Mom received many similar pieces of correspondence," Andrew said with pride. "She answered every one of them. She was grateful and supportive. She felt it was the least she could do. My brothers Leo, Ralph, and Joe and my sister, Rita, were all in Europe fighting. Rita was a Canadian Army nurse. She was often on the front lines. My youngest brother Bud signed up. He was off to boot camp."

Bud, Andrew's youngest brother, after the war ended. AFC

UNITED STATES PACIFIC FLEET
AIR FORCE
BLIMP SQUADRON THIRTY ONE

MRS. J. FLANAGAN,
JACQUETTE RIVER.,
NEW BRUNSWICK, CANADA.

DEAR MRS FLANAGAN.,
EVERY NIGHT I LISTEN TO THE PRISONERS OF WAR FROM TOKYO, JAPAN,
ON THE SHORT-WAVE RADIO HERE AT THIS STATION.

TONIGHT I HEARD THE FOLLOWING MESSAGE FROM YOUR SON ANDREW FLAN-
AGAN, 25YRS OF AGE WHO WAS A RIFLE-MAN WITH THE ARMY IN CHINA.

"I AM IN GOOD HEALTH, AND DO NOT WORRY TOO MUCH AS I WILL BE AL-
RIGHT. I RECEIVE YOUR LETTERS AND PARCELS OK. HE ALSO SENT RE-
GARDS EITHER TO THE FOLLOWING MEN OR FROM THEM. IT WAS NOISY
ON THE AIR AND I DID NOT HEAR WHICH WAY HE MEANT THE REGARDS,
BUT THEIR NAMES WERE AS FOLLOWS. ALFRED E____?____. , ABE
DRISCOLL, JOHN KILLERAN, ELBERT ____?____ , JOSEPH LANDREY.
LOCATED AT ONTARIO. GOOD LUCK AND GOD BLESS YOU ALL. ANDREW.

TRUSTING THAT THIS LETTER WILL GIVE YOU A LITTLE CONSOLATION
IN KNOWING THAT HE IS ALIVE AND WELL, AND IF I SHOULD HAPPEN TO HEAR
HIM ON THE AIR AGAIN, PLEASE REST ASSURED THAT I WILL NOT HESITATE
TO LET YOU KNOW AT ONCE.

YOURS FOR A QUICKER VICTORY.

Stephen G. Spicer S2/c
U.S. Navy.

PLEASE ADVISE ME OF RECEIPT OF THIS LETTER.

Letter from Seaman Second Class Stephen G. Spicer, US Navy,
to Andrew's mother. AFC

The following is an example of the thank you letters Mrs. Flanagan sent. She saved every letter she received and copies of every thank you she sent.

To: United States Pacific Fleet
Seaman Second Class Stephen G. Spicer
U.S. Navy

I cannot express the joy that I experience reading the words my son speaks. It is like he is speaking to me. I hear him. I thank you with all of my heart.

Many good people on the west coast sent the same message. I cherish each and every one of them. I hear Andrew's voice every time I read one.

God Bless you and the entire alliance. We will defeat the evil in our world.

In closing thank you for fighting for your country. I am sure your mother is very pleased with your efforts.

Most sincere appreciation,
Mrs. Mary Emma Flanagan and
James Flanagan

In July 1944, Andrew's parents also received a copy of a letter that Albert Murchie's wife got from California. The Murchies lived in the area and knew the Flanagans. The local families always forwarded letters of broadcasts that mentioned other local boys to their people.

Wife of Albert Murchie, age 34
Rifleman, Canadian Army, China
Nash Creek, New Brunswick

My dear Mrs. Murchie;
    The following message was heard by short wave from

Radio Tokyo on June 1, 1944, when messages were sent from American and Canadian prisoners of war in Japanese camps. The message was apparently written by your loved one, and I hope it is genuine.

I have been listening in steadily to these broadcasts for about a year and a half, taking these messages in shorthand and relaying them to relatives of the men interned. To date, I have written about 2870 letters, and all expenses are borne by my husband and sister. I am employed during the day and can work at this hobby of mine only at night and on weekends. For that reason I sometimes fall behind in my correspondence, and I hope the late arrival of a message will be excused. The messages from the Japanese camps are heard several times a day, seven days a week, the best reception being midnight, Pacific war time, while those of the German camps are heard on Saturday night only. I write letters until 3.00 a.m. every day.

The message for you is as follows, and I hope it won't be long before your loved one is back home with you again, safe and sound.

"This is Rifleman Albert Murchie, Royal Rifles of Canada, broadcasting from a prisoner of war camp in Japan to my wife and family and relatives of Nash Creek and other parts of Canada. I want you all to know that I am well and hope you are the same. I received parcels from you Helen. I also received letters from you Otto (?), Also Earl (?) and the rest of the family. I have written you also. Trust you got them. Must state that the boys from home who are with me are all well, namely, Abraham Driscoll, Eugene Lapointe, Joseph Frenette, Andrew Flanagan, Manny Hickey, Niles Dempsey, John Killoran, Alfred Elsliger, Joe Landry, and Leo Pitre. Must sign off now with love to all of you. Hope to join you again. Good luck and Cheerio. Your husband, Albert Murchie,"

Sincerely,
Cecelia McKie

Andrew said the POWs all had to follow the same basic script, so most of the broadcasts were very similar. Not all the boys were able to send messages by radio, so that was why many of the local boys were mentioned.

In mid-October 1944, winter came early in Tokyo; things were freezing up again. Andrew and the other POWs in Camp D worked on a number of other ships being built and some in dry dock. That Christmas was another where the POWs didn't receive a Red Cross parcel. Andrew said he hadn't seen parcels in months, nor had he received news from home. Food was bad, even worse than previous months. "We lived on 3 oz of rice a day. I guessed that I tipped the scales at slightly over 75 pounds. But there was a spirit in all of us, including the dying. It gladdened us to hear that some ships that we had built had sunk."

In reference to a poem written by his friend and fellow POW Fred Elsliger, Andrew said, "Some boys had exceptional talents, which they shared to make our stay a bit more tolerable." Fred shared a true, horrifyingly humorous poem that Andrew believed encapsulated the tenacity of the Canadian soldiers in the Far East.

The Siege of Hong Kong
by
Alfred J. Elsliger,
Jacquet River, New Brunswick

'Twas at Valcartier, Quebec, one cold October day
That we received our orders to pack up and start away.

We marched down to the station in a cold and drizzling rain,
Then bade good-bye to friends nearby and stepped on board the
   train.
That journey to the west coast was rather boresome trip.
We arrived in Vancouver, then got on board a ship.

We were going to see new country, everyone seemed gay.
There we joined the Grenadiers and started on our way.
They just came from Jamaica, we from Newfoundland,
We all told different stories, we were a jolly band.

Our destination was obscure, but little did we care,
As our ship, an Old Newzealander, was taken us somewhere
We knew not where we were going
   What's more we did not care,
Where we went or what we did
As long as we got there.

We stopped in Honolulu, but didn't stay there long;
Our officers then told us we were going to Hong Kong.

We landed in Manila next, another large seaport,
Some thought the journey ended, but our sojourn
There was short.

Next landing was at Port Kowloon across from old Hong Kong.
The streets were lined from end to end with
Cheering waving throng.
We marched to Nanking barracks next about a mile away
And there received the welcome of the proverbial "flowers of
   May"

The place was like a festival with sport and food galore;
At night the grounds were lighted from the lights along the
    shore.

What pleasant hours the boys spent there
In canteen drinking beer;
Both noon and night, day in, day out
We'd find Tom Thompson here.

The Barbers shaved us as we slept
And gave us haircuts too,
As Coolies kept the camp in shape
We had no work to do.

But happiest hours must have an end;
Two weeks — it wasn't long
When we broke camp and crossed the straits
To fight on old Hong Kong.

Just two short weeks of gaiety
For all of us and — well
'Twas just a touch of Paradise
Before we entered hell.

We fought a noble battle
But at such terrific cost
That even though the fight was brief,
A lot of lives were lost.

We next moved to Stony Hill
And stayed there overnight.
From there we went to Repulse Bay
To join another fight.

With Royal Rifles, Middlesex and Hong Kong Volunteers
The Royal Scots, East Indian and Winnipeg Grenadiers.

We fought together valiantly, that time at Repulse Bay
But the Japs outnumbered us and we were forced to move away.
We fought till we were famished with the hope that ground we'd
    keep
For hours on end the battle raged, we fought on in our sleep.

We fought while death in its worst form
Struck men who would not yield;
But when Jap re-enforcements came
We had to leave the field.

Then finally the finish came
That fateful Christmas Night
The stars, as over Bethlehem
Were shining clear and bright.

"Peace on Earth" cannot prevail
While bombs and shells abound,
And hundreds of our comrades brave
Lie dead upon the ground.

We knew we were out numbered
By a thousand men to one
We felt our case was hopeless
Ere that fight had scarce begun.

So we handed in our rifles
And our ammunition too,
Buried our dead, then went to bed
('Twas all that we could do).

And now we're in a prison camp
And live on rice and rats,
It might be worse, if Japs were Chinks
We'd have to live on cats.

But I'm fairly optimistic
And some day hope to be
Back in the land of Freedom
At home as I used to be.

There'll be Merrier Christmas greetings
Than we utter this Yuletide last;
We'll have happier Christmas meetings
When the evils of war are past.

We'll sing a merrier Christmas anthem
And cheerier New Year's song
When we think of that Christmas battle
On the Island of Hong Kong.

Fred made it through the Battle of Hong Kong, survived the sinking of
a hell ship and suffered out the war as a prisoner until he was repatriated
in October of 1945. After being home for only one month he died in an
automobile accident. He was changing a tire on the side of the road when
he was struck by a car.

"New Year's January 1, 1945 — I didn't think I would see that New
Year's alive," Andrew would say later. "There was nothing left of me; I was
worked to the bone. If the war didn't end in 1945 I knew I would be dead
by next New Year's. The Japanese couldn't feed or keep us. So rumours
were that they would use us POWs for medical experiments as a measure
to reduce our numbers. Apparently we weren't dying fast enough."

Andrew said he saw a memo posted in Nip on the guards' wall with
the headline "KILL THEM ALL." Apparently that notice was posted at

all POW camps under Japanese control. It outlined what to do in the event that the camp could no longer keep control of the POWs.

At the end of January Andrew sent a card home:

Dear Mother, Dad and Family

I hope this short message finds you all well, I am still enjoying good health, had a letter from Ralph some time ago. Hope to see you in the near future. Don't worry.

Love Ando

Once again Andrew lied to his parents about his health. However, he said he knew his mother had probably figured out that he lied to her to protect her from anxiety.

Andrew said,

It was very cold for the rest of the winter in 1945. I was sick all the time. I wish the guards didn't take my diary for that period. I was literally too sick most of that time to remember what had happened. I did remember another ship sank…right in the harbour. It was rumoured that three other ships that we previously worked on sank at sea. The Japs were angry when we all *hurrahed* as we saw the fourth ship under the waves, sunk in the port. We'd like to believe that it sunk because we messed with the rivets, but the Japanese were so anxious to get that ship out they also made mistakes. They didn't send inspectors around as often as before. One POW crew said they just tacked a few rivets on a number of steel plates on the bottom of the doomed ship. Without doubt we got the blame for the sinking anyway, which made many of us proud. We saw the sinking as our "badge of courage."

After the fourth ship launched by the POWs sank in Tokyo harbour on April 9, 1945, Andrew and a group of other POWs were ordered to stand at attention while the Japanese beat them with bamboo staffs. They asked if the Canadians had sabotaged the ship, but no one admitted to tinkering with the rivets. "I was sure the Japs would kill us on the spot if we admitted to screwing with the structural integrity of the boat," Andrew said. The Canadians survived yet another close call.

Shortly afterward, their ordeal entered a new phase.

Chapter Eight

Sendai #1 POW Camp
and the Coal Mines

On April 9, 1945, a fire swept through the camp at the shipyard. The flames jumped from one building to the other, burning the old shacks like kindling. Andrew got most of his belongings out, but many POWs lost what little they had, he said. By then, the area had become the scene of much destruction as the Allies dropped bombs quite frequently and many parts of the city were set afire. Andrew recalled that "the Americans were bombing the shit out of Tokyo." Andrew asked Joe Landry if the bombings frightened him. He recalled Joe answering, "Ando, I'm not scared of nuttin' anymore."

Joe had changed a lot from the fifteen-year-old kid he was when they were captured. "Joe became a man far too fast," Andrew reflected. "I used to pretend not to be afraid, hoping to calm Joe. I guess he grew up believing me. He grew into what I pretended to be. It was a shame that he was in a POW camp. Joe was a man by 1945 and he took care of me as I got weaker. He reminded me of my little brother Bud. I supposed Bud was all grown up then."

After the last ship sank, the POWs were marched to the train station where they boarded for parts unknown. As they travelled, the western setting sun was to his left; therefore the right had to be east, so Andrew assumed they had to be heading north. The next day 198 Canadians arrived at Sendai #1 POW Camp at Yumoto on the northeast coast of Honshu. "The railroad ran through the middle of the camp," Andrew said. "As I disembarked at the coal mine camp the guards inspected my diary and confiscated the book from September 1943 to April 1945. I never got it back, but I'd remember most of it, and I vowed to tell anyone who would listen."

The Canadian POWs were split into work parties and told that they would be miners at the Joban coal mine until the war was over or they were dead. The food situation there was worse and they had no cigarettes. At least at the docks they could trade with the foreigners from time to time, Andrew said.

Andrew despised working in the mines. He later talked about the job. "I believed I would die there if the war did not end quickly."

My first shift in the mine was terrifying. We were loaded on a trolley at the top of the mine shaft. As the train entered the shaft everything went black. I panicked and began to suffocate. I jumped to my feet and hit my head on the low overhanging top of the tunnel. I fell off and landed hard on the side of the tracks. I could see the light from the opening in the tunnel. I ran towards the light. I dropped to my knees as I emerged from the depths. My hands were red with my blood. I apparently had cut my head. A Japanese guard ran over shouting at me to get up. I explained in Nip that I fell off the train. He put his rifle to my back and, speaking in Nip, ordered me to walk. We walked the entire length of the tunnel until we came to where the other prisoners were hacking at the coal seams. I tried to get relocated to work on the surface, but as soon as the Japanese understood that I had a fear of working underground, they made me stay there.

By then, Andrew's health was rapidly declining, he said.

One morning a few weeks after we arrived in Sendai I got a scare when I woke. A tooth fell out of my mouth. I pushed it back in but eventually it dropped out. My teeth, in general, were in bad shape. They were loose and I had many decays. Toothaches were the norm. Finn tells me that my dental problems were probably caused by the lack of proper nutrition. Finn was our Canadian commander at

Sendai. He thought that I might have had scurvy and told me to eat more fruit. That would be fine except there was very little fruit around there. I knew Finn was right but I also figured that all the beatings I got at the mines had also loosened my teeth.

By late spring 1945 Andrew was very sick. All there was to eat were small rations of rice. He worked six days a week in terrible conditions. Deep in the shaft, the POWs had to follow the coal veins. Sometimes the vein was only a metre high, other times it could be six or more metres high. On several occasions the cave ceiling fell in, killing or injuring many underneath the rubble. When they could, the survivors dug out the dead POWs and gave them proper burials. A number stayed buried deep in the mines due to the large size of the cave-ins. "I was claustrophobic all my life, but I only fully realized I had the condition when I came to the mines," Andrew later recalled. "I hated that place beyond any place I had suffered as a POW. As a youngster, my brothers locked me in a steamer trunk for a gag. Ever since that day I hated tight restricted places. The mines were driving me insane." He said they used a pick and shovel to loosen the coal and loaded it onto a push cart, which they pushed to the rail. Then it was moved up to the surface and dumped. The Japanese civilian guards worked the POWs very hard.

At one point Andrew overheard Joe Landry tell Lieutenant Finn that Andrew was very sick and that Joe was worried about him. "Joe pegged it. I didn't feel right. I didn't feel anything. I didn't give a shit anymore. I didn't even think about food or home or anything anymore." Finally, something encouraging happened.

I found an old Japanese newspaper in the summer of 1945. I couldn't read Japanese fluently, but I could understand some words and phrases. I thought the headlines read that Germany was defeated. I hoped so. The Japanese would know what hurt was when the entire Allied army attacked Nippon. A civilian worker told me that it was true, Germany had quit the war. I remember thinking, "Hang on Japan; the fun has just begun." This news raced through the mines and the camp faster than a cat with cans tied to its tail. Within an hour all the POWs were talking about it, speculating what would follow in Nippon. It was all the encouragement I needed. I felt like I caught my second wind. Perhaps I would make it home after all.

By August 1, Andrew was extremely thin and was too weak to be working, but he was forced to labour anyway. The younger soldiers like Joe helped him out. "Our clothes were rags," Andrew said. "It was over a year since we got a new piece of clothes. All I had were tattered old rags to wear. My shirt was over four years old. I sowed what I could, but the cloth was rotten. It didn't matter underground because it was so hot we were working in our G-strings."

Andrew said they felt two earthquakes, one on August 6, the other on August 9. However, they may have been manmade, matching the dates the atomic bombs were dropped on Hiroshima and Nagasaki. "Rumour had it that we had a bomb so powerful that we could wipe out an entire city with one detonation," Andrew said. "I hoped it was true. If so, the war would be over soon. If not, I would be dead soon."

Andrew spoke of a bad civilian guard named Suzuki, who they nicknamed Mad Dog, and a Japanese soldier they called Frogface. "I got many beatings from [them]. Frogface was ugly. He looked exactly like a frog. His face was flat, his eyes bulged out from the sides of his head and his mouth was a horizontal slit with no lips. He was cruel too."

We got another, more severe beating from Suzuki and Frogface during the second week of August. Joe Frenette from Jacquet River and me were working in a very tight place. We were following a coal seam which was only four feet high. We were deep underground where it was extremely hot. We wore only a G-string to cover our privates. The runoff water steamed and burned to the touch. We came out to the gallery to cool off. Suzuki and Frogface accused us of not working hard enough. Suzuki hit Joe with an iron bar. I told him in Nip that we were working very hard. He turned on me with the iron bar and hit me many times on the body. When I fell he struck me across the face and broke my nose. Blood shot out of my nostrils. Joe helped me back to our work place where he reset my nose. I heard Frogface tell Suzuki that he was doing a good job as we limped away. He told him the Canadian POWs deserved a beating for what the Americans did to Japan. At that time Frogface probably knew about the devastation caused by the atomic bombs. We were unaware of it.

At Sendai, the POWs heard only rumours about the status of the war or the atomic bomb. It was noted that the Japanese were being very quiet, as if they knew something.

Unbeknownst to me, Japan surrendered verbally because of the atomic bombs. Aside from rumours about a powerful bomb, I knew very little. I did not know that the Japanese surrendered. Suzuki must have known when he beat me. Camp POW leader Lieutenant Finn told me in July to report any beatings I got. Every time I did, Suzuki beat me harder the next day. That went on for many days. I knew Finn reported the abuse to Frogface and Frogface must have told Suzuki, who beat me more for telling on him. Suzuki told me in Nip that he knew I told on him. Suzuki told me to shut up about beatings or he would continue to beat me more. I reported him anyway. That night I dreamt about home where I had Suzuki between the house and the barn. I sure enjoyed punching him, even if it was only in my dreams. I wished my brothers would appear sometime when the shit was beating on me. They'd put an end to it in a hurry.

Back home Andrew's family knew more about the war ending than he did. On August 17, they received instructions from Colonel H. Ellis, Director of Repatriation, about communicating with Andrew now that the war was over.

> To: Next of Kin of E30353 Rfn. Flanagan J.A.
> Now that victory over Japan has been attained, we are looking forward to the return of those who have been prisoners of war in Japanese hands.
> Communication during these years of internment has been very difficult, but it is now possible for us to forward for you a letter which will be flown to Manila and placed in the hands of the liberated prisoners at the earliest possible moment.
> This letter includes a form and airmail pre-addressed envelope.

His parents were also informed that special airmail had been set up for the liberated POWs to send letters home. Soon afterward, the Canadian POWs in Japan learned that they had survived: their war was over. However, their personal battles went on.

Chapter Nine

The War Ends

On August 20, 1945, Andrew woke up early. His nose was still sore from being hit by Suzuki with the iron bar. The dried blood that dripped from his nose overnight caused the jute bag he was lying on to stick to his cheek. There was no noise outside. The usual morning bustle and Japanese shouting of orders to get up were missing. The ringing of silence in his ears heightened Andrew's instincts that there might be trouble. There was much talk in the camp about the Japanese killing the POWs if they were defeated. Andrew hoped that was not happening.

Tentatively he got out of bed. When Lyle Dempsey from Jacquet River asked him where he was going, Andrew replied, "Something's wrong. Come on outside with me." There were no guards in the watchtowers or on the ground. An eerie silence was broken by a hollow thump as the wind pushed the main gate against its metal stop post. The gate was wide open. Lyle exclaimed that there wasn't a Japanese soldier around, then yelled, "The war is over! I'll never eat rice again!"

The Japanese government had surrendered on the fifteenth but the Sendai Japanese guards hadn't told the POWs; they just disappeared on the twentieth. Andrew later said that he and Lyle whooped *yee-haws* until everyone was awake. It took some time for all of the POWs to fully comprehend that it was over...they were going home. "The boys walked around smiling for the first time in a very long time," Andrew would say with a look of satisfaction. "I wondered if I could find Suzuki. I had a little something for him. I'd punch the guy silly if I could have caught him that day." He'd punch his bony fist into the palm of his other hand as he spoke.

Shortly after the camp was awakened an American airplane flew very low over the camp, dropping notices proclaiming that the war was over and soon the Americans would be dropping food and supplies into the camp. They asked the POWs to take cover in a safe place, such as a bomb shelter, when the food drop started to avoid being hit by the barrels. The notice also requested that they stay in the camp until the Allies arrived. "That afternoon several of us went outside the camp anyway. I wanted to find Suzuki. The local Japanese were scared of us. I was not interested in those poor folks. I asked many in Nip if they knew Suzuki. Several told me he went over the hills. He had gone to hide.

"At the market we got fruit and other food. Back at camp Lieutenant Finn gave us hell for leaving. Water off a duck's back as far as I was concerned. To hell with 'em, the war was over and me taking orders was also absolutely over." Andrew would end his story with a tone of certain defiance.

It took a week or more but the food barrels finally reached Sendai. In the meantime, Andrew and a few fellows from his hometown went outside the camp and picked up three pigs, which they slaughtered and cooked up for the camp. Andrew remained unhealthy, recording that he had a boiling fever. POWs in Japanese prison camps were being liberated after the surrender of Japan.

Most POWs in the Japanese system throughout the Pacific were in deplorable physical shape, many being on the verge of starvation and death. Jonathan Vance, editor of *The Bamboo Cage*, writes about POWs in one area but the same conditions were prevalent at every Japanese POW camp. "When Allied forces arrived at the camps of Java in August and September 1945, they found thousands of malnourished prisoners clinging to life."

On August 29, Andrew wrote:

> This morning at 5:30 a B-29 flew over camp. It came from Saipan with food & clothes for POW camps. I later found out that it unloaded at a local airport and supplies were transferred to a B-17 which dropped them down on our camp. Ten oil drums at a time the parachutes of every colour

opened, approximately 50 or 60 drums landed in the middle of the camp. Today there was everything from matches to cherries. We didn't mind staying there when there was plenty of food available.

During Andrew's videotaping in 1990, he stopped reading his diary at that point and told a story of the first food barrels dropped over the camp. "We were in the bomb shelters as soon as the barrels began to drop out of the plane. The colourful parachutes opened and the barrels landed all around us in the camp. We waited until the last barrel landed, then we rushed out like kids on Christmas morning. There were tins of juice of all sorts in the first barrel that I opened. Two Aussies stayed out on the tracks that ran through the camp. A parachute broke over one fellow. The barrels plunged to the ground, and flattened the poor guy. The oil drums were heavy, full to the brim with food and goodies. We let the Japanese civilians have the barrels that landed in the jungle or up in the hills. We didn't chase any outside the camp. We had plenty." Andrew smiled at the lens as he thought of how great it was to have so much to eat.

Andrew said they had so much that it was comical to see the fellows trying to share their bounty, but everyone had so much that they didn't have to share any longer. During the previous years as POWs they always shared whatever they had. Some fellows got extremely sick when the barrels of food first dropped. They gorged themselves, eating far too much. Andrew didn't get ill because he was too sick to overeat. At the beginning of September Andrew was on sick parade and was tended to by medical officer Lieutenant John A.G. Reid from Toronto.

Later, all of the barrels were gathered and the contents were issued to the men. Andrew wrote that he received cigarettes, chocolate bars, three packs of gum, four bars of soap, and American clothes. He said they received all of the things they hadn't had for a very long time, including clothing, new razor blades, shampoo, and real soap. On the evening of the first drop Andrew wrote that he was certain they were the cleanest people in all of Japan. "What a luxurious feeling it was, lying on a clean blanket, dressed in clean clothing, smelling like roses and holding my full

Andrew Flanagan, at left, on September 9, 1945. US National Archives.

belly," he said. "It would be a while before the Americans could get us out of there. It didn't matter when we had plenty of everything and we knew the suffering was over."

One night around that time, Andrew said, he dreamt about his grandfather Andrew Donnelly. When he awoke he wondered if he was still alive. He was ninety-seven when Andrew last saw him before the war. It was at that point that it struck him that he had missed many momentous events. He probably would have taken them for granted if he had stayed home from the war.

On September 2, Andrew visited friends at the nearby Tiro camp. He had dinner with Matias, a HKVDC POW, and Wardie Hamilton from Blackland, NB. They had both been shipped to Japan after Andrew had left Hong Kong. They told him that Fidele Legacy had died in Sham Shui Po. "My friend Fidele Legacy, who was in bad shape the last time I saw him January 1943, died shortly after my last visit to him. Matias told me Fidele

Pencil sketch of the snapshot by Jillian Flanagan depicting her grandfather, James Andrew Flanagan, packing his meagre belongings on his last day as a POW. He weighed sixty-eight pounds. AFC

traded a pair of sunglasses that I had given him for stationery to write a letter home. Matias didn't know if he lived long enough to write the letter."

On September 4, Andrew recorded that a B-17 supplying POWs crashed about five kilometres from their camp that morning. It was the second crash in a week. Ten servicemen were killed in the first one, thirteen more in the second crash. "Those 23 American airmen died trying to deliver us supplies," Andrew said. "They flew very low to avoid dropping their cargo outside the camp. I felt indebted to those men. All I could do was send them a prayer."

By the end of the first week of September, Andrew was feeling better. The POWs left the camp at will, and travelled wherever they wanted to go. The train was near the camp and Joe Landry and Andrew took a two-hour trip to visit their friendly boss from the shipyards; they had supper at Akiba's house in Onahama. The house was a traditional Nippon building with paper walls. They sat on the floor to eat at a coffee table and the food was very good. The family only spoke Japanese, but by then Andrew was mostly fluent. He said he drank too much sake, and didn't remember getting off the train back at the camp. Apparently, Joe carried him.

On the eighth, Andrew wrote that 600 POWs waited on the docks for the American fleet, while US planes dropped food on the docks for them. Andrew also sold or traded with civilian Japanese. He sold two Japanese blankets, boots, and a belt earning him ¥150, which he used to travel and buy other things.

Back home, on September 8, Andrew's folks received another letter from Colonel George H. Ellis with additional airmail forms. The letter also included instructions detailing how other family members and friends could write to the POWs. The POWs did not receive many of their letters because they moved out before the correspondence arrived. A few months after he got home, Andrew received a letter from his brother Bud, written on September 10. It had been rerouted from Japan back to Canada through the army. In the letter Bud said he wanted to meet Andrew on the west coast when he got there from Japan… "The invite was too late, but I found Bud anyway," Andrew would say.

On September 9, Andrew wrote that at 0500 hours he and his fellow Canadians left Sendai camp and boarded a train in the camp yard. He recorded that all of the towns and cities they passed through, except one small town, had been completely destroyed by bombs. At 1600 hours, they arrived at Yokohama and were met at the station by an American band playing music from home. "As the US Army band welcomed me I felt proud, but also guilty. I thought of all those who would not hear a welcome again. I didn't think that I was alright just then. My feelings of grief seemed to trump all excitement about the war being over. I wondered what the other fellows were thinking. I hoped I wasn't crazy."

Road transport took the Canadians to the nearest American headquarters where, Andrew wrote, they had them "sign papers galore." They ate supper at the American headquarters. "There was plenty to eat. I took a nice long hot-water shower. Put on all new clean clothes. We were then whisked off to a waiting landing barge where we were transported to the *Monitor*. It was a big ship. We slept there."

The next day, Andrew wrote that he was up at up at 0500 hours. He and the other Canadians left the *Monitor* on a transport barge and then boarded the USS *Wisconsin* in Tokyo Bay. It was huge, he wrote, displacing

45,000 tons. Andrew was put into the ship's hospital. He had a large infected boil on his hip and weighed in at sixty-eight pounds. The onboard dentist filled some of Andrew's worst decayed teeth and extracted two that were beyond repair. He told Andrew that he had a gum infection from not eating properly and that his loose teeth should tighten up as he got better nutrition. He gave him penicillin to treat an abscess and told him to wait a month, then go to a dentist back home. That would give his teeth and gums time to heal with proper nutrition.

Within a few days, Andrew weighed more and was packing on the fat.

I thought of eating all the time, which was an improvement, compared to the last few months in camp where I was too depressed to care about anything. I'd be as fat as a little pig if I didn't slow down. I woke up, screaming in Nip that night. I woke half the ward. I had a horrific nightmare where the devil and five of his cohorts were torturing my dead friends. I recognized the five evil spirits as five Nip guards who most frequently beat me and my friends in POW camps. Suzuki, Frogface, Horseface, Tojo, and the Kamloops Kid. I'd hoped to find those fellows before I left Japan. I offered to stay and help search for them when I first got to the American headquarters. They told me I had done my part. They would catch the war criminals and bring them to justice.

While on board the *Wisconsin* Andrew wrote the following letter to his mother and father:

Sept. 10, /45
Dear Ma & Pa

We left our POW camp in Sendai yesterday morning by train, arrived at Yokohama at 1600 hrs.
Met at station by American army band playing etc. supper at army HQ. Slept on board Monitor, left it this morning

and boarded this battleship. I am in hospital on board, boil on my hip and to get more rest. Last word I had was a card from Dr. Smith dated Feb. I received it in July. All was well at that time. I hope that you are all in good health yet. We quit working in coal mine on August 20. One cannot express in words our feelings on that day.

Were we glad? We took over the camp about 20th then things really came our way. Small planes from the USS Lexington, found our camp in the hills and dropped us food, supplies, cigs & Medicine, fresh meat & bread etc.

Well folks the war is over and I am on my way, when I get to Jacquet River I don't know, I do not know where or when we go from here.

Anchored off Yokohama today, about 115 Canucks on board so far & 2400 of a crew. Excellent food and plenty of it.

Joe Frenette, Landry, Lyle Dempsey, are on board this boat. Alfred Elsliger is aboard a hospital ship, he's got a burnt foot. Fidele Legacy died in China, early in 1943. Quite a number of boys from JR will not return. Since I've been a POW I received 5 letters or cards & 1 parcel. Last letter I had from Bud he was in Montreal. I sent a cablegram from HQ in Yokohama last night. I hope this finds all in good health, give my regards to friends, & I'll soon be with you

PS please excuse writing as I do it in bed. Please do not write me till I forward a permanent address.

Till then,
Cheerio

Ando

The following was written on the back of the letter:

The US Navy has promised our commanding officer, an American that they'll land us on the other side of the pond. We know very little about news since we received no newspapers except a few old Nip papers in /43.

We worked in a dockyard here (Yokohama) until May of this year, when this city was flattened by air raids, we were then shifted to a coal mine in the north.

I'll give you more dope on things when I see you. We are getting looked after the very best, all kinds of cloths, the best of food and plenty of it.

The Canadians received US Navy uniforms for clothes to replace their remaining rags, which were completely done. Andrew said they looked good all dressed in white. "American sailors treat us with the utmost respect and kindness," he wrote. "Many show us a good time." When the US commander introduced the Canadians to the crew over the PA system, he said:

"Our guests, the Canadians on board today, were fighting the Japs six hours after they attacked Pearl Harbor. We will do all we can to help these soldiers and make their stay here comfortable."

On September 12, they left the *Wisconsin* and were transported across Tokyo Bay on a landing barge. After arriving at Kisarazu Airport they departed for the Pacific island of Guam on a C-54 transport plane. "We flew over Tokyo for 25 minutes," Andrew wrote in his diary. "There wasn't much to see as about ninety percent of the city was burnt & destroyed. I saw ships in the harbour and the burned out structure of the shipyards where I had worked. We hit air pocket over the ocean that made me feel kinda creepy. We flew at 5000 feet, where I could see white fluffy clouds beneath us. There was a lovely sunset at 18:10 hours."

He later said that when he saw the beauty of that sunset and felt it deep within his soul he knew he would be all right. "It had been a long time since I had considered anything beautiful. I thought right then and there that I would always feel some guilt for coming home without many of my friends, but I would live with it as I knew they'd want me to. I would try to see the splendour in my life. I owed it to my fallen friends."

Andrew wrote in his diary, "We ate supper on the plane at 19:30 hours. We were over Guam at 2300 hours. We remained at 5000 feet, circling for over 1 ½ hours. It was raining very hard. There were nine other planes at 500 foot intervals below us. We had to wait until they landed before we did at 2400 hours. It was a perfect landing."

After landing they filled out papers and then had lunch. Andrew went to bed at 0300 hours and was up at 0730 hours. Each of the ex-POWs was given a small package of toilet articles, bars of soap, cigarettes, and candy. "A very nice nurse was taking care of all our needs," Andrew said. "Guam was beautiful. I walked around town for something to do. It was a very interesting place. I sent a cable home to Mom and Pop that day."

He wrote in his diary, "The next day I received $5 from Sister Molly who was with the American Red Cross. Sister Molly was not stingy with confectionery of all kinds. McNamara of the USA Army also outfitted me with a pile of clothes."

"I felt like a VIP," he said, "the way I was treated there. Everyone was very kind to me. From their talk, I gathered they knew we had it extremely hard as POWs. T/5 Edward G. McNamara, the US Corporal who gave me clothes, also helped me drink a pint of whisky." At this, Andrew would smack his lips like he could still taste the liquor. "McNamara also gave me his Sacred Order of The Golden Dragon card that he earned by crossing 180 degrees longitude. He said 'I earned it in '41 when I first crossed.'"

On September 15, Andrew was still in Guam. He had a chest X-ray and weighed in at seventy-five pounds. That was the heaviest he had been in over three years. The next day, he left the American Navy field hospital and boarded the USS *Ozark* at 1300 hours. Before leaving he had to get a pair of shoes from Joe Landry. "I lost my shoes somewhere after drinking the whisky with McNamara. It was a good thing Joe had a few pairs. McNamara said I took my shoes off at a house where we were being entertained," Andrew laughed.

The same day, half a world away, his dad received a special notice in the mail from the army:

OVERSEAS CASUALTY RESEARCH
Date: September 16, 1945
Reg. Number   E30353   Rank Rfm.
Name Flanagan J.A. Flanagan
Nature of Casualty: Safe in Allied hands 9 Sept 45
...Condition Fair.

SACRED ORDER OF THE
GOLDEN DRAGON

Know ye, that __T/5 Edward G. McNamara__

on the __1st__ day of __July__ 19 __45__

aboard the __U.S.S. GRIMES APA 172__, Latitude _____,
Longitude 180°.00, having been inspected and found
worthy, was initiated into the
Sacred Order of the Golden Dragon

人史走邪 KOON HEE FUT CHOI
Ruler of the 180th Meridian

Membership card from the Sacred Order of the Golden Dragon. AFC

"My whole family rejoiced when Pop read the letter to them. Mom cried. Four years of endless worry and the unknown as to where or what had happened to me was now over. She was a tough woman and I was sure she would never cry while I was expected to be strong. Those few words, 'safe in allied hands,' removed the black cloud of distress and replaced it with tears of joy. If she only knew how much I had missed her," Andrew said with tears in his eyes.

He continued, "The next day we set sail from that pretty island. I experienced beauty and felt a host of good feelings, more frequently with each passing day. I felt really good. I couldn't wait to get home. I planned to buy a new car with my back pay."

He wrote, "On September 25th we docked in Pearl Harbour Hawaii. It was a lovely place. I went on shore in the evening where I bought four cartons of cigarettes for $1. I drank my first beer in almost four years. It cost 10 cents and tasted nasty." The next morning they sailed from Pearl Harbor.

On October 2, Andrew wrote that they were approaching the coast of North America in thick fog. The ship's foghorn blew every ten seconds. "It was so foggy there that I could hardly see across the deck. The distant sounds of other ships' horns were eerie, and got on my nerves a bit," he said. "A welcome-home ship met us in San Francisco harbour. A beautiful band played while loads of waving girls and WACs cheered for us. We got off Ozark onto a ferry, which took us to McDowell Island in the San Francisco Bay. A tall 60-foot-high illuminated sign at the island read, 'Welcome Home, Well Done.'" At Fort McDowell Andrew listened to a few speeches. The Canadian lieutenant governor and consulate were also there. Andrew said he got paid $20. Dressed in US Navy uniforms, Andrew and an American friend named Davey went to town. "Davey and I had a swell time in town. Many pretty girls. Some thought I was a sailor in the US Navy. I told them the difference. A big fight broke out at the hotel where we were drinking. I sat that one out," Andrew said.

On October 3, Andrew left Fort McDowell by ferry for Oakland where he and fellow ex-POWs boarded a Canadian vessel. He said there was one man to one seat. "What a luxury. We even had a steward catering to us. I thought of the hell ships and the suffering that my comrades endured. Images of my friends that I left behind popped into my mind without control," he reflected.

In Eugene, Oregon, Andrew saw a brand new Kaiser-Frazer car. It was two-toned blue and white with more chrome than the King's Rolls-Royce. What a beauty, he thought. He decided that he would buy one just like it when he got home. He and a crew of friends spent an evening in a tavern in Portland.

On October 5 they arrived in Seattle, Washington, where they boarded the *Princess Alice* heading to Victoria, BC. "There were thousands of thronging folks out to meet us in Victoria. It was a tremendous reception. The MPs had a hard time parting the crowed for us to board the waiting buses," Andrew wrote in his diary.

On the next page of Andrew's diary was a neatly written note from a lady friend.

Do you think you will remember us when you get home Andy. You know the house on Edgeware Rd. Hope you have a good welcome when you get home.

Sincerely,

Eleanor Mars

"I would say no more about that angel of mercy, except that yes I would remember 1466 Edgeware Road, Victoria, BC," Andrew said with a smirk and a raised eyebrow.

"We were bused to a large hall. As we entered, the place erupted in quiet applause. People stood and clapped without saying a word. You'd think the Pope just entered church. They were handing out fancy welcome cards." The cards read as follows:

The Mayor

The Mayor, Reeves and Councils of Greater Victoria have great pleasure in extending to you a sincere and Hearty Welcome to Victoria (Vancouver Island) Capital of British Columbia
On your repatriation from the hands of the enemy.

We sincerely wish you and yours the best in health and welfare in the future.

During his videotaping Andrew held up a yellowed piece of newsprint dated October 5, 1945.

THE ROYAL RIFLES COME HOME

The men of The Royal Rifles of Canada who this day return to the country are to be welcomed with stirring emotion as men who are returning out of the past and from the dead. Nearly four years have gone since they were enveloped in catastrophe — a catastrophe into which the whole world was almost drawn. They once again set foot upon the soil which has been far from them in space, farther in time, and farthest of all in experience. Now after their long voyage, the space no longer separates; after the slow passing of the years, there is no longer the separation of time; after the miseries and anxieties inflicted upon them with resourceful cruelty, they have been restored to the security of their Canadian homes.

Of all the numberless and varied reunions of this war perhaps none will be as touching as this. For upon these men, in a primary and unequalled way, the impact of the enemy's advantage descended. They faced the enemy when the enemy was never stronger, and when the resources of Allies were never more unequal. The mission on which they were sent represented a failure to anticipate the tragedy of a small garrisons standing in remote isolation against the irresistible tide. For these men of the Royal Rifles there could be no fate but death or imprisonment. And to the imprisoned, nothing less than the slow reversal of the whole immense tide of war, could bring deliverance. These men were the first Canadians of this war to enter battle, and the last to be freed from the enemy's hands.

Their return is made a moving experience, not only by what they suffered, but by the spirit with which they bore the weight of such odds. Some picture of what they had to face and fight in the sudden attack in December 1941 has been given by Maj-Gen C.M. Maltby, the commander of the Allied garrison at Hong Kong. He has told how the men of the Royal Rifles had no time to learn the ground over which they had to fight. Their primary task was the seaside defence of the colony but they were actually required to carry out local counterattacks against the Japanese advancing from the landward side.

The Canadians had to turn and fight their way up the slopes in a desperate effort to dislodge the enemy. They fought gallantly in heavy gear up steep hills, and fought to exhaustion after suffering heavy casualties. The odds were six to one against them but the battle lasted 17 days. And they were unaided by air power or by the navy.

Something of what they have suffered in the years of imprisonment that followed the men themselves have told with reluctance. We have learned of their prison food, monotonous, meagre and repellant; and of the shrewd procedures of humiliation and torment with which the effort was made to break body and spirit; and of the precautions taken to withhold from them all information of the world lying outside the misery of their prison limits. Their attitude towards what they have endured is expressed by one of their numbers. "I don't want to talk about Jap treatment or brutality," he said. "It's over and I want to forget it. We've had enough."

Their reluctance to speak should now aid them in forgetting their harrowing experiences, yet what they have suffered, and their spirit of courageous endurance, ought to be remembered forever in their honour.

And we ought to remember not only the sacrifice and courage of those who have returned but of those who will never return to their own soil. These men, too, though they can only in our hearts come back, ought not to be without

their remembrance and their welcome. Though they lie, at our orders, in a land remote and strange, they yet have their true place in the land which is their home:
They mingle not with their laughing comrades again;
They sit no more at familiar tables at home.
But where our desires are and hopes profound,
Felt as well-spring that is hidden from sight, to the innermost heart of their land they are known
As the stars are known to the Night.

Andrew said, "This was a true article. It paid tribute to those who stand to forever in Hong Kong. Many returning men would not speak of the horrors they had endured. That was how they handled the memories. I, however, felt compelled to do the opposite. I felt a hint of revenge when I told people about the cruel bastards who hammered on me and my friends. People should know. Japs that committed war crimes should be punished. War is hell."

On October 6, Andrew went to town and had a swell time with Cliff Flanagan from Dalhousie. They visited people in the country, stayed the night and went back to camp at 0800 hours. "As I entered the camp gate a young soldier ran up behind

Rifleman Leslie Firlotte, Royal Rifles of Canada, 1945. Courtesy of the Firlotte family

Gravestone for Rifleman Ron Kinnie, Royal Rifles of Canada, at the Stanley Military Cemetery, Hong Kong. Courtesy of the Kinnie family

me and hit me in the arm. I'd sworn after being a POW that I would never be hit by anyone, without retaliating. I swung around and punched that son of bitch as hard as I could. He fell to the ground laughing at me. 'It's me, Ando, your brother Bud!' 'I didn't recognize you,' I said, half ashamed for hitting him. 'You're all grown up.' He said it didn't hurt. It was great to see Bud, but I felt a slight bit cheated. I didn't get to see him grow into his boots. I eventually came to realize that many other intangible things and events were robbed from me while I was away. Bud told me he was on his way to Japan (to get me) with the Canadian Army when they got the news that Japan had surrendered. I wished I had had a few like him around when Suzuki or Frogface mistreated me."

On the eighth Andrew wrote that they boarded an eastbound train and they were in Calgary at 1900 hours, where he had a good time. The next day, Andrew met a clergyman in Regina whose last name was Branch, from Bathurst, NB. He was in an air force uniform. Andrew also recorded that he met Helen Armik at Brandon and attended a big reception in Winnipeg put on by the city.

At 0600 hours on the eleventh they arrived in Toronto to another big reception. About eighty Royal Riflemen got off there. Toronto was a big town and Andrew said he had a swell time there. The next day Andrew left Toronto for Montreal where he changed trains and boarded the Ocean Limited heading home to Jacquet River. He said he sat with Leslie Firlotte from Jacquet River and they talked about all the things they were going to do when they got home. "Between Montreal and home I thought of the excitement we all felt four years prior. I also thought about my friend

Ron Kinnie and the rest of the sons who wouldn't see their mothers at the train station. Fifty miles from home, I began to read Ron's diary entries leading up to the Battle of Hong Kong. I remembered crossing Canada and the Pacific Ocean with so much wonder and anticipation. That was then. On the last leg of my journey home I carried a different anxiety." Ron had been in HQ Company earlier with Andrew and during the battle they had fought side by side. "A hell of a good fellow, brave to the very end, Ron was. He died a few hours before the end of the Battle of Hong Kong." Andrew wiped his wet eyes.

Chapter Ten

Home from Hong Kong
and the Later Years

On October 13, 1945, Andrew wrote his final wartime diary entry: "Exactly 4 years to the day since I last saw home." Andrew told his homecoming story with exact details, like it had just happened the day before.

> The train jolted to a stop in front of the Jacquet River station. At the door I jumped out with my packsack and duffle bag. There was a huge sea of people waiting there. Over 20 of us Royal Rifles of Canada soldiers disembarked. I saw Pop in the distance leaning on the fender of my old Ford, lighting his corncob pipe. It looked like my brother Roge was asleep behind the wheel of the parked vehicle. Mom intercepted my course through the crowd. I didn't want to stop hugging her. And I didn't want anyone to see me cry. I told Mom not to worry about me. Heck, I said to her, I'd never want or need ever again for the rest of my life and I'd never do without again, I promised. That was a promise I planned to keep.

Andrew kept that vow. He had little regard for money, one of the side effects of starvation, he would say. He only wanted the things that he was denied as a POW, like freedom, food, shelter, clothing, and beer.

"Mom had a boiled dinner waiting for me at home. All my family came to visit and eat. Food had never tasted so good. I ate until my belly was sore. We drank beer and exchanged war stories late into the night," Andrew said with pride. Five of the Flanagan men and their sister served in the army during the Second World War. Andrew's mother said that she

Joe Landry, Andrew Flanagan, George Steeves, and
Alfred Elsliger, Royal Rifles of Canada, 1945. AFC

had six to worry about throughout the war. Andrew's other brother Roge had a heart murmur, and couldn't pass the army medical when he tried to enlist. Just as well, Andrew said, as their father needed a man at home to run the farm. Of the six of them who joined the army, all served overseas except for their youngest brother, Bud, who enlisted shortly before the war ended. They all made it home and each one had an amazing story to tell.

That first night home, Andrew said, each sibling in turn told their wartime stories. Brothers Ralph and Joe were with the Calgary Tanks and the Princess Pats. Ralph told about going to Sicily and then into Italy, where he met up with Joe. Their accounts of certain battles when they went head to head with scores of German panzers (tanks) made Andrew wonder how they ever survived. As much as these stories impressed him, Andrew was most proud to hear about their boxing championship in England before they crossed into Europe. While hundreds of thousands of Allied soldiers were in England training for the day when they would fight the Germans, a boxing championship was organized by the Allied forces, where all of the troops would compete to become the golden-gloves winner among the fighting men in England. For many months, divisions from just about every Commonwealth nation competed. They narrowed the field until the two best fighters were pitted against each other in a final fight for boxing supremacy. Yes, Ralph won by a very close margin, barely beating his brother Joe. "I was so proud to hear that story that I felt like taking them out between the house and barn to see if they'd really improved that much," Andrew said with a laugh.

Andrew's only sister, Rita, had crossed the English Channel like the fighting brothers, as a nurse in the Canadian Army. She told stories of administering first aid near the front lines and carrying a pistol with her that she was capable of using in a fire fight. She was often face to face with Nazi infantry. "Rita was scared of nothing and a damned good boxer too. If there was a women's boxing division, I am sure she would have walked away a champion, too," Andrew said proudly.

His brother Leo was also in Europe with the Corps of Engineers. They built the bridges that got the Allied equipment across the many rivers and streams on their way to Berlin. Leo talked about building bridges

Andrew's sister, Rita, wearing her nursing sister uniform, and fellow nurse, Gertrude MacMillan. Ken McIvor

on one side of the river while the enemy fired at them from the other side. As the bridges were completed the enemy would retreat to the next bridge, which they usually blew up. The cycle continued until the Nazis were defeated. Bud, the joker, told several funny stories about local fellows. One guy, whom he did not name, thought that going overseas meant crossing the Bay of Chaleur.

Then it was Andrew's turn. "The room hushed as I spoke of the unthinkable events I endured in the Far East," he recalled. "I didn't have brave fighting stories in me that night. I told with tears in my eyes the sad stories of how each of our local boys died. These were our friends, boys who had sat at our table before the war. I stopped speaking when I saw my always-composed mother reach for a handkerchief." Andrew slid both index fingers across his eyes as he spoke.

Andrew changed the subject to his grandfather Donnelly who had died while they were away fighting the war.

"I had trouble sleeping that first night home. My own bed felt foreign. Oh, it was as comfortable as I had remembered, but perhaps it was too comfortable. I got up and drank another beer by myself. The house was silent. I thought of all my friends who would never ever get to enjoy the quiet of their own homes again. Later, I closed my eyes to a continuous movie film of flashing faces in my mind: Fidele, Arthur, Raymond, Ron, John, and so on."

The next day he started back to work with Dr. Smith. When Andrew was overseas many local fellows had wanted his job, but Dr. Smith was true to his word and kept Andrew's job open until his return. The following week Andrew spent a few days getting badly needed dental work. The dentist told him to continue eating fresh fruit because some of his teeth were still loose. "I had awful toothaches as a POW and when I returned home. I was hoping that my teeth were the cause of my rough nights. My teeth were fixed but I continued to have restless sleeps. I woke often screaming in Nip as the echoes of my war revisited me. Drinking helped me fall asleep, but as I sobered the nightmares returned." On November 2, Andrew was involved in a car accident in Campbellton with his brother Leo. Andrew's left eye was smashed and several front teeth were knocked out. He pushed the teeth back in place but his dentist told him the next day that he put them in the wrong places.

"On November twelfth my friend and former POW, Fred Elsliger, was killed in a different car crash near his home," Andrew said. "He was changing a tire alongside of the road when a fellow who may have been drinking hit him. It was a very sad day in Jacquet River. Poor Fred went through the battles of war, survived the sinking of the *Lisbon Maru* hell ship and the torture of years as a POW only to get a month of freedom at home. I miss Fred."

When he reported for duty, after his disembarkation leave was over, Andrew was immediately transferred to the Fredericton Military Hospital. "I made my way to what would become known as the DVA (Department of Veterans Affairs) Hospital in Fredericton. They kept me there for a few months, partly because of injuries I sustained in the car accident, but mostly because of the wartime mistreatment I suffered in Japan," Andrew recalled. "I was hungry that first evening in the hospital. At suppertime a very businesslike ward aid placed a food tray under my nose. She whipped the warmer cover off the plate. I smelled that pungent smell. I envisioned slimy maggots infecting the white rice. I projectile vomited halfway across the room as the doctor walked in. He told her to remove the rice and tray and to bring me some Canadian food. 'Never serve an ex-Japanese POW rice,' he warned her as he apologized to me."

On January 9, 1946, almost two months after he was admitted to the hospital, Andrew gave and signed his wartime deposition. "It detailed my mistreatment as a POW. Captain J.C. Van Horn signed as a commissioner for taking affidavits. My briefing was presented to the Government of Canada and sent on to the Supreme Commander of all Allied forces where it was read and submitted as evidence at the Japanese War Crimes," Andrew said, feeling that he had exacted a bit of revenge.

> I should have read my diary before giving my deposition. But, like rice, I could not stomach to look at the words they contained. It took years before I could read my entries. I forgot many horrible events. Perhaps I didn't want to remember them. Years after the war the memories came back to me like the rising tide crashing against the cliffs at our beach. They were more clear and vivid than ever. Some nights I jolted awake and sat up as straight as a picket to what I could only explain as an alternate reality where I thought I was still a POW. Somewhere deep in my mind things came back to me that I really didn't want to know. I remember things so wicked and inhuman that even I refused to talk about. I hoped someday to forget about those grisly memories.

A week later Andrew reported to the Fredericton Army Depot. He was immediately transferred back to Quebec. On January 29, 1946, Andrew signed his discharge certificate, relieving him from active service in the Canadian Army. "I received an honourable discharge! I bought a bottle for the train ride home," he concluded.

By the end of February, Andrew had written to Ron Kinnie's mother. "I hoped she got the letter. I was not certain about the address. I couldn't find the strength to drive down to Ron's place. At that time it was just too sad a journey for me to take. I didn't give her the picture sealed with his blood. I hid it deep at the bottom of the iron box where I kept most of my wartime items and papers." In April, Andrew received a letter from Ron's mother:

April 3rd 46
Dear Mr. Flanagan

Just a few lines this time, we rec'd your letter of Feb. 20, it
had been to so many different Post Offices. Am glad you were
with Ron as a pal, and hope you will soon be well yourself.
If you get this letter, write, perhaps you will be able to visit
up here some time, more particulars next letter.

Mrs. Arnold Kinnie
Ron's mother

In the first week of March, Andrew received a statement of his War
Service Gratuity showing that he was to receive $998.19. Andrew jumped
into his old Ford and drove out to Stewart McAlister's in Jacquet River.
Stewart owned the local Ford dealership and also sold Kaiser-Frazers, the
elegant car that Andrew had seen in the States on his way home. He asked
Stewart how much a brand new Kaiser-Frazer cost. "I want a two-toned
blue and white one with more chrome than paint."

"Expensive; it'd run you a thousand," Stewart answered.

"Would you take $998.19?" Andrew asked as he tossed the gratuity
statement on his desk. Yes, he would. But he had nothing in inventory.
Stewart said, "It could take up to a year to get one here. You know the
war is barely over, it takes time to ramp up car production." As Stewart
filled out the papers he wrote in large red letters, "RUSH! A return POW
Veteran needs transportation. He has a taxi license and needs that car to
earn his livelihood." Stewart studied the gratuity statement for a moment
and pointed out that they would pay Andrew $76.76 a month for fifteen
months, not $998.19 all at once. Stewart looked at him and said, "Ando,
you just bring each cheque into me for the fifteen months and that car
will be yours." Andrew recalled, "My Kaiser-Frazer was in within six
weeks. I totally demolished it in a head-on collision within a year, but I
gave Stewart every gratuity cheque. We were on a drunk the night of the
accident. I was taking Joe home when an oncoming car didn't dim his

lights. Oh, the bastard dimmed when I was blinded by his bright lights and in his lane. I don't know how we didn't get hurt. I bought a brand new Ford Super Deluxe from Stewart the next day." Andrew smiled as he ended his car story.

Andrew wrote Major-General Ernest G. Weeks, Adjutant-General at National Defence Headquarters, advising him that he was willing to go to Japan to testify at the war crimes. Weeks wrote to district command asking if Andrew would be prejudiced. "Can you imagine, wondering if I would be biased against the people who beat and humiliated me for years. Darn right I'd be," Andrew declared. In April, Andrew received a carbon copy of Weeks's message to the Americans.

Canadian Military Attaché,
c/o Commander, Cdn. Army Staff,
2222 "S" Street N W,
Washington 8 DC, USA

E-30353 Rfn FLANAGAN J A

Canadian Army

Ref File: M.A. 16-2-11 G/13 Feb 46

2. Herewith duplicate original and certified true copy of Deposition, reference
Japanese War Crimes, received from soldier.
3. For transmission to the War Department Pls.
(E G Weeks)
Major-General,
Encl.   Adjutant

His deposition was sent to the Supreme Commander Allied Powers, General Douglas MacArthur. Throughout 1946-47, he received correspondence and signed affidavits to confirm his deposition as his testimony at the Japanese war crimes trials.

The Kamloops Kid was tried for war crimes by a military tribunal, and was convicted and sentenced to death. However, the verdict was overturned on appeal. As a Canadian citizen he couldn't be prosecuted for war crimes committed by an enemy army. Andrew was infuriated: "The Kid was getting away with his crimes. I was so angry at that news I thought about going to the Far East to get him myself. And I didn't mean to testify, I meant to get him." The following April Andrew got good news; he didn't have to go to Japan to get the Kamloops Kid. "I read in the newspaper that the Kamloops Kid would be no more," he said. "He was tried again, this time on the criminal charge of treason. He was found guilty, and on August 27, 1947, he would be executed by hanging at Hong Kong's Stanley Prison, ironically, only five miles from where the bastard beat so many of us. Normally I'd feel bad for the loss of a human life, but I didn't consider that thing human."

Then, the prosecutor for Sendai area war crimes requested affidavits and debriefings from J.C. Frenette and Andrew. They both gave testimony under oath against Suzuki, the Mad Dog. In October 1947, Andrew received a letter titled "Interrogation of Repatriates — Far East JA Flanagan," including a copy of his statement against Suzuki:

Statement of J.A. Flanagan — I was severely beaten with an iron bar about August 1945 by one Suzuki, Jap civilian guard and boss. I received about 30 beatings from Suzuki. [Everything else was blacked out.]

"I hoped Suzuki would get the same as the Kamloops Kid," Andrew said. In December, he got a letter thanking him for his information and informing him that Suzuki and his accomplices had been sentenced to thirteen years in prison at the war crimes trials. "Not near enough. I'd like to be his guard for a day. It'd be my turn then to beat. I hoped I'd never see him again. Given the opportunity, I'm sure I would have killed him."

Andrew continued struggling to reintegrate into peacetime life. He spent the rest of 1946 "just trying to adjust to civilian life. I hoped someday to drop the images of horror that visited me at nights," he said. He wasn't alone. Bud Sweet's son Charles recalled his father's experiences after the war.

> We hardly ever talked about the war but some things crept out from time to time. It is my understanding that Dad was shot in the back, across the shoulder blades as we always saw the scar from the wound. [While he was] recouping in the hospital [at St. Stephen's College] the Japs raided the hospital, bayoneting patients in their beds. When it was his turn to receive the bayonet he rolled out of bed, took off running from post to post, then was shot in the arm, falling through the door followed by the Jap who then bayoneted him through the stomach. He was about to do it again when Nursing Sister Kay [Christie, a Canadian] said to stop and he did stop.
>
> Every Christmas Eve Dad would vanish and as kids we were always curious about where he was. I guess he retreated to his bedroom. Years later one Christmas Eve he asked me if I would join him in having a drink, and said it was his anniversary. I said, Dad, you're wrong, you got married in June. Dad said no, it was fifty years ago on Christmas Eve they cut off his arm. What an awakening it was for me...I was speechless.

Around September 1948, Andrew met his future wife.

> I walked into the hall under the church where the basket sale was underway. It wasn't my idea to go to the basket social, but my brother Bud said Clara Shannon might be there. I had an eye on that girl and my brother knew it. A basket sale in our rural Maritime community was a tradition brought over from the old days. In early fall, the single girls made

baskets, that was to say they decorated picnic baskets and, with their mothers' help, filled them with baked goods. The objective was to raise money for some good cause. The girls saw it as a chance to meet a beau.

As I descended the steps into the basement I saw Clara's basket placed on the bidding table. Some little snip up front bid a dollar. I shouted, "One hundred dollars!" The priest choked on his words as he accepted my bid with an affirmative cough and a hand wave. I got Clara's basket and I got her attention.

Following the auction I sat with Clara, Mrs. Shannon and her aunt Lena. We ate thick slices of homemade bread smothered with wild strawberry jam followed by chocolate cake with tan coloured coffee icing and plenty of other food delights. How I wished I could have taken that basket back a few years to Sendai POW camp. I hoped Clara was as good a cook as her mother. After the lunch I gave them a drive home. Clara sat for a spell in the front seat of my car. She was gorgeous.

Andrew recalled their conversation. "I am leaving tomorrow for Bathurst Mines where I will have my first teaching assignment," Clara said. "I am so excited I can hardly wait. The mines are quite remote; far in the woods behind Bathurst. I doubt if I'll get home much."

"I'll be busy too with work for Dr. Smith," Andrew replied, "and I am buying a hundred acre farm from the Ultigan brothers, when I get the money." After this brief chat, they said goodbye. As Clara closed the door, she said, "Goodbye, soldier boy."

Sometime later, Bud told Andrew that Clara had returned. He drove over to her house and "after my third pass in front of their farm, I gathered the courage to turn in. I jumped out of my car and caught a glance of Clara as I walked around the corner of the large farmhouse. She was behind the shed, peeking through tall thistle plants." When Andrew knocked on the door, Mrs. Shannon opened it and told him to come in and have a seat.

She called from the back door, but there was no response. Bert Shannon, Clara's father, was hauling on his barn boots at the side door and told Andrew to come out to the barn. "I'll show you my new horse." In the horse stable, Bert reached into the hay trough and pulled out a bottle of B&B whisky. "We each took a big slug. It burned all the way down, and just as I thought it was cooled, a hot spot hit my stomach again. I guessed it must have been Bert's barley corn." Leaving the barn, Andrew saw Clara behind the thistles, but much closer to him. Without a sound, she mouthed "soldier boy."

"I mouthed back, 'Saturday.' I saluted her as I jumped in my car. She sure was pretty. When I returned on Saturday, Clara was on the front yard swing waiting for me. And so began our lifelong relationship."

Andrew recalled their wedding day.

It was a cold December 26, 1949, at −20 °F the night before. I was worried my car wouldn't start in the morning so my brother Roge went out every hour to start the old Super Deluxe. I had to be at the church for 8 a.m. in Belledune. Driving past Clara's house, I saw the horse and sleigh was gone. She was walking into church as I drove up. She turned quickly toward me. I pulled my felt hat down over my eyes...could be bad luck to see her that morning before we were married. I lifted my hat just in time to see the priest's black Ford dead ahead. I missed it, barely.

The reception at Clara's parents' house was great. The food was so plentiful. I wished I could send it back, back to the time we did without. How odd, but somehow fitting; this best day of my life should follow the anniversary of the worst day, namely, the fall of Hong Kong. I felt a sudden spike of joy at the reception. 'I am all right now,' I said to Clara. I saw in her eyes she was oblivious to the real meaning of my statement. I didn't explain. I just said that I was very happy.

Andrew also recalled, "I scared the heck out of Clara that night when I screamed in Nip in the middle of our first night together. I heard my mother tell Clara the next morning that it happened from time to time. Mom coined my night terrors as 'Ando's war.' The nightmares were consistent. The devil and the five bastards that beat on me in camp were hurting my late friends. The cruel hobgoblins were always Horseface, Frogface, Tojo, Suzuki, and the Kamloops Kid. I knew I would fight those bastards for the rest of my life."

His wartime experience remained present in other ways. In June 1949, a cheque arrived, issued to him, in the paltry amount of $56.40. That was his slave-labour pay. It worked out to less than five cents a day. There was no mention of an apology from the Japanese government. Then, on September 25, 1950, Andrew received a letter regarding his war-service pension.

> The Canadian Pension Commission
> Dear Sir:
>
> As provided by the Pension Act, the Commission have reviewed your case and decided the question of your entitlement to pension. Their finding is attached.
> In the opinion of the Commission, your disability from Avitaminosis with Residual Effects is 20% in extent and you have no assessable degree of disability from Haemorrhoids. Pension, therefore, is being awarded you of 20%.

In October 1950, Andrew got his first pension cheque. It wasn't much but it helped when combined with the $30 a month he earned working for Dr. Smith. He knew the extra money would come in handy, with his first baby on its way. On November 24, their oldest daughter Joanie was born. "She was beautiful, like her mother," Andrew recalled.

> By March of '51 we knew there was something seriously wrong with Joanie's health. She took epileptic convulsions.

Andrew Flanagan's Second World War medals. AFC

The doctors didn't know what was wrong; their treatments were not working. They suspected brain damage at birth. A year later, the following March, Joanie was in a Montreal hospital. The doctor told us he released some fluid from Joanie's brain. She was stable and would most likely live. For how long, he did not know, but he knew she would not be normal. Joanie continued to have convulsions, but not as frequently. That spring Clara, Mrs. Shannon, and I took Joanie to St. Anne de Beaupré. Joanie's convulsions had returned as bad as ever. I believed my wife's faith in St. Anne had somehow worked. Joanie will likely out live me and all medical predictions of a short life. She never again suffered convolutions after her visit to St. Anne de Beaupré.

Andrew wrote to the government when he didn't receive any of the medals that his fellow ex-POWs had. In 1955, Andrew finally got his war medals. They included the 1939-45 Star, Pacific Star (Overseas Service Far East), and Canadian Volunteer Service Medal (CVSM). Later, he received the Hong Kong bar to his CVSM.

In 1956, Andrew's mother passed away. "A remembrance day I shall never forget," he said. "How I regretted losing those five war years away from her. If I forgave the Japanese it was because of her. Goodness and sacrifice for others was the only way to describe Mom. Thinking of Mom was a preoccupation of mine while I was a POW. She didn't know it but thoughts of her pulled me through my darkest hours overseas."

In 1962, Andrew was hospitalized again at the DVA facility in Saint John, NB.

My lungs had been bad ever since I worked in the coal mines in Japan. I was walking to work when I took a fit of coughing. Dr. Smith's house was a quarter mile down a lane from my house. A late winter snowstorm blocked the road. By the time I reached Smith's house I couldn't breathe. I fell on the floor. Dr. Smith called my brother Roge to come get me. Roge hitched the mare to the woodsled and raced over the snow banks to get me. A car waited for me when I got to the main road. They rushed me to the Bathurst hospital. By the time I got there my face was black from lack of air. The doctor stabilized me and put me into an oxygen tent.

The next day he sent me by ambulance to the DVA hospital in Saint John. After several weeks of intensive care, I was well enough to move to a regular ward. Unfortunately, during my recovery period I had a coronary heart attack. That complication kept me at the DVA hospital until late spring. When I got home I felt much better, but from that day forth I spit a quart of mucus daily, for the rest of my life. I was told that emphysema combined with coal miners' lung caused the chronic condition.

"I'm lucky to be alive," he concluded.

In March 1963, Andrew's father died. "Once again I couldn't help but think of the five war years I lost with him," Andrew said. "A big burly man, he was slow to anger but your worst nightmare when he was upset. Don't get me wrong, he loved to argue, especially politics, but mostly it was all in fun. He was a man of his times. He didn't cuddle us much as children and didn't do housework. I guess that was why I was so surprised at what he said to me after I got off the train on the day I returned home from Japan. He said, 'I'm proud of you, son. I'm glad you're home safe, and I missed you.' I'd miss him too."

In 1963, Dr. Smith had a stroke.

> We sent him by ambulance to Bathurst Hospital. Dr. Thompson sent him off to the DVA in Saint John. They did all they could for him, but he was completely debilitated by the time he returned home. He required constant care. I met with his legal representative and trustees who appointed me as his guardian. I hired Pat Ultigan and Nurse Mary Shannon to help take care of the elderly man. Pat and I were friends and neighbours for years. He was a veteran who fought in Europe. He was awarded the Golden Oak medal for bravery in a battle in Holland. Pat told a funny story about how he earned his bravery medal. He was manning an anti-aircraft gun, located at the end of a port jetty. He didn't hear the evacuation order. Unbeknownst to him he was all alone fighting. He shot down many German airplanes until the Germans finally called off the attack. Pat would laugh and say he wasn't very brave, just a little deaf.

On May 20, 1965, Andrew's longtime employer died. "Just before he died he asked if the mistress of torture was in the room. That was how he referred to Mary Shannon, the kindly nurse, who checked on his condition daily. I stared at his lifeless body. His mouth dropped open and his blue eyes were dull. I saw a lot of dead men in my day; his death affected me differently. What a remarkable scholar he was. A graduate from Oxford, holding many degrees, a doctorate in English and an architectural degree as well. A World War One veteran, he understood my situation. He was one of the few who knew why I drank," Andrew said sadly.

In May 1966, Andrew inherited $20,000 and Dr. Smith's house. After many months of searching for the perfect spot, Smith had chosen Irvine Ultigan's cow pasture as the place to build his retirement cottage. The high cliffs, blue water, and Appalachian Mountains across the Bay of Chaleur reminded him of a beach area he had frequently visited as a lad with his father back in England. He drew his own blueprints for an English-style two-storey cottage with a large veranda overlooking the bay. Twelve old-style, one-foot-square panes made up each of the twelve large windows in that building. Opening the front door you'd step under a twelve-metre exposed Douglas fir beam, which complemented the craftsmanship in the building. Clara and Andrew loved the house and were grateful for the bequest.

"I owed large medical bills and I managed to attract a few fairweather friends that year. Cronies of course. It took just a year to spend the cash," Andrew said unashamedly. Dr. Smith also left hundreds of thousands of dollars to the University of Leeds in England. He also bequeathed his library of rare old books to the University of New Brunswick.

In 1967, Andrew's fourth son, Stephen Percy, was born and named after Dr. Smith. Although he was not related, Stephen had a long head like Dr. Smith, Andrew recalled. "I hoped he would be half as intelligent." Andrew had eight children, four boys and four girls.

In April 1967, Andrew's brother Roge died. "He was the first of my siblings to go. He was in a coma for months following a bad car accident." Their father had left the farm to Roge with the stipulation that when Roge died he would leave the farm to their nephew Joey. A cleaning lady and her three boys lived at the house with Roge. She cooked and took care of the house while the boys helped Roge around the farm. When Roge's last will was read, the family learned that he had left everything to her.

In 1972, Andrew joined the Corps of Commissionaires and got a job as a minimum-wage security guard. He worked at the hospital for a while and then at the salmon pools in nearby New Mills. It was seasonal work but it paid for his beer, he would say. He worked with the Corps until he retired at sixty-five years of age.

On December 26, 1974, Andrew and Clara celebrated their twenty-fifth wedding anniversary. A neighbour organized a party at her house with all of his family and friends attending. "Clara and I renewed our vows. Father Trudel handed me the holy cup, I took a sip, and offered it back to him. He laughed and said, 'take a good drink Andrew, you deserve it.' I thought at first the priest was referring to my war service, until I turned to see my youngest children rolling on the floor in a three-way fight. I guess the priest figured I earned an extra swig of the wine." Andrew laughed.

Andrew planned to enjoy his retirement. "I was done working. I got the old age pension, 90% veterans pension and a small Canada pension (just enough to buy my beer). I was not bored. I read a lot of Smith's books. I liked the way he always corrects Shakespeare's grammar. Reading *As You Like It*, I noticed a correction in pencil, followed by 'tut tut.' Shakespeare wrote 'Fairwell'; Smith corrected it to 'Farewell.'"

By then, grandchildren were arriving. "I had the privilege of taking care of Luke, my daughter Kathy's baby boy and my first grandchild. Kathy returned to school so I babysat the child. Luke was a fiery little redhead. We had a great time together."

Andrew still suffered from the effects of his wartime service. "My lungs were worse than ever. I filled a spittoon in a day," he recalled. "Coal dust and years of abuse were catching up to me. I still woke up at night screaming in Nip, fighting a battle without end. My family told me I was worse when I drank whisky. Drinking beer helped me fall asleep. Whisky made me fightable."

His children all had first-hand experience with his night terrors. "At first when they invited a friend to spend the night, they would get embarrassed by my nighttime yells. Then it just became a lark. When a new person slept over they waited for my nightly hollers to scare the heck out of their

Andrew Flanagan remembers his fallen comrades at a cenotaph in Sussex, NB, during a reunion of Hong Kong veterans, circa 1984. AFC

guest. Sometimes I woke up to their laughter. Didn't stop their friends from coming over, or stop them from getting into my fridge for a lunch." Christmas Day in the Flanagan home was confusing; the excitement of the season was subdued by the anniversary of the fall of Hong Kong on December 25, 1941. The Christmas message was often overshadowed by tales of heroics, death, and suffering. Andrew's stories of friends who died during the battle and the circumstances surrounding their deaths were as much a part of the yuletide tradition as singing Silent Night. Andrew's accounts often ended with the wipe of a tear from his eyes, quickly followed by a defiant look. Unspoken but clearly understood was that he had the right to shed a tear for his lost friends and all their suffering.

In 1988, at a Hong Kong veterans reunion, Andrew heard that he could get his military records from DVA. So he wrote to the National Archives of Canada requesting a complete copy of his files. In fall 1988, Andrew received a large brown envelope weighing three or four kilograms. The contents were archived copies of every scrap of paper they had in his army records. Andrew already had many original papers, but that package provided missing copies or connections to other correspondence. When combined, these scraps of paper told Andrew's story.

Reunion of veterans of The Royal Rifles of Canada. AFC

In December 1989, Andrew and Clara celebrated their fortieth anniversary. "A grand party was planned for that summer, when all my children and grandchildren were home. I was rather tired of the parties and that sort, but I did appreciate the forty years that Clara and I had shared. I was a lucky man. All my children were educated and mostly were on their own. Joanie would always be my little girl, whom I cherished. I was also confident Clara would be by my side in my time of need."

In October 1991, Andrew's youngest brother, Bud, died. "He was much too young to go," Andrew said in a low tone. "I still regret not being with him when he became a man during the war. There was something unfair about my youngest brother's death, happening before mine. Bud lived in New Hampshire. Regrettably, I was too old and feeble to attend Bud's funeral. I sent some of my children in my car."

Christmas continued to be a time of reflection for Andrew. "I thought of my friend Ron Kinnie, who died three hours before the Battle of Hong

Kong ended. Fifty years had passed by the Christmas of 1991. Fifty years since I became a prisoner of war. I never forgot my fallen comrades, or the ones who had passed on since. It seemed there were only a few of us left, only a few to keep the memories alive."

In 1948, Andrew had joined the Hong Kong Veterans Association. Each year they held a reunion that was attended by hundreds of Hong Kong veterans.

> I had hardly missed one in forty-five years, but our numbers had dwindled to only a handful of attendees, but our children continued to be active. It was time to pass it on to the younger ones. Lest We Forget! I and most Hong Kong veterans took their families to the reunions, it was a trip, but it was also a chance for my kids to meet other veterans. Some vets talked about creating a commemorative association to continue our work when we were gone. Joe Landry and I often travelled together to the reunions. Poor Clara got to drive us around and put up with our goings on. Joe was still doing all right, but his nerves were bad. His wife left him some years ago. She was a nice girl, but had a hard time with the night terrors and other problems that Joe, like most of us, inherited from Hong Kong.

1992 was a long, hot summer for Andrew. Sometimes he could hardly breathe and he spent most days on the veranda where the air was fresh and the view was spectacular. However, by Christmas 1992 Andrew was very sick. Although he would not admit it, Clara knew. His eyes were bad and he could no longer read. He felt weak and tired, and said he didn't even enjoy a beer anymore. "Soon it will be time to go. Honestly, I've no fear of death," the old soldier said. "I've been to hell before. I continued to have night terrors with the same tormentors as always. If I didn't find peace in this world, I [will] find it in the next. That's a promise I aim to keep."

Andrew died on February 27, 1993. At 79 years old, Andrew had lived a full life, a good life. He said that he hoped he had lived a life that made his

The Battle of Hong Kong

J.A. Flanagan
Jacques ... 43

Dec.6th, According to news dispatches Japan will be at war with Great Britain & her Allies, also the U.S.A. in the near future.

Dec.7th, Japan appears to be more aggressive, today we were ordered to leave Kowloon and take up our positions on the Island of Hong Kong, left Kowloon at approximately 1400 hrs, arrived at Tsa Tam barracks about 1700 hrs, that is H.Q. Coy.

Dec.8th, Reveille @ 0430 hrs ... for war, Battle order, everyone standing by @ dawn we hear war has been declared, Japs bomb Tai Tak airport & set fire to the hangar & put it out of commission ... attack ... with bombers ... + Jubilee building + machine gun ...

Dec.9th, Reveille 0430 hrs, Duplessie & I take up our position on side of ravine between Tsa Tam & Lie Moon, and see more bombs dropped on Lie Moon. bombed Lie Moon

Dec.10, Hear of fierce fighting at Border, bombed Victoria.

Dec.11, Japs have broken through at Border.

Dec.12, Rumours the R. Scots & Punjabis are retreating from Border to take up position on Island.

Dec.13, Today I saw them shelling & bombing Sea Wan.

Dec.14, The same as yesterday. God scare 1st shell burst in front of Tsa Tam 2000 ...

Dec.15, Rumor tonight that a large force of th enemy tried to land at Sea Wan were successfully repulsed with heavy casualties inflicted on enemy.

Dec.16, Snipers are becoming more numerous on Island. This morning Ruachie, Duplessie & I went down to Chinese shacks about 300 yds. in front of H.Q. for some lumber to make our black out more effective at officers mess, took us on half hour, had to dodge about 15 shells, as this was my 1st shelling in open & ...

Dec.17, Heavy shelling of Island from ... and bombing of Sea Wan & city many fires started in city.

Dec.18, Today the shelling and bombing was severest yet, about 2000 hours shelling was at its heaviest all centred on Sea Wan & Lie Moon, about midnight I heard the enemy were landing at Sea Wan.

Dec.19, Heavy battle going on up on Mount Parker, Sgt Roy, Alfie Mills and Cpl. Vincent, and quite a few more of my comrades either captured killed up there, Lieut. Williams was killed this morning. Artillery opened up on enemy on side of mount in front of Tsa Tam H.Q., ordered to go to Tam Villa about noon, I went out with some ... Major Macaulay's equipment left it at Tam & returning to Tsa Tam about 1600 hrs got Major Strand & Lt. Col. Knap, each my own kit bag, toward H.Q., with Pitan, left this with Major Macaulay ...out 2000 hrs and slept in trench in front of Tam Villa for short intervals up at 0400 hrs next morning.

Andrew's account of the Battle of Hong Kong. AFC

Dec. 20. At daybreak he left to go to Repulse Bay, however we were held up on the way by enemy intensive machine gun fire took shelter in a small trench, forced to get out of there, went up on the hills & then back to Pam Villa, fallest through peach socke.
Left P. V. at 08.00 lunch

Dec. 21. Anoea attack led by Major TG Macaulay from Pam Villa towards Tia Tam reservoir, ran into about fifty japs at turn in road by Pettol dump heavy battle there, we had several killed and quite a few wounded, I went from there back to Pam V. to get an ambulance, & was sniped at quite a number of times by machine guns & rifles, one bullet gave me a flesh wound on finger, went back in ambulance to join the Major, by that time to we had cleaned up on enemy it that than in road, we started on to next turn in road & as we came around it, an enemy car was coming towards us, two B. Carriers were with us equipped with Vickers the Vickers opened up on car & the enemy took into the woods & we presumed they entered a house a short distance from where they abandoned their car, as our mortar gun went into action the second shell from it landed in the centre of the house, we saw several army behind house towards the road which ran under the reservoir, & I saw several H.K.V. took up a position on side of road watching covering road under reservoir, very soon we were rewarded by seeing several trying to pass the _____.
The Major Macaulay went towards where the car was abandoned and was badly wounded in arm, then a few minutes later Lieut. Peters of th H.K.V. was killed there,

We then went back to turn by petrol dump a H.K.V. officer asked for some stokes to put Red Hill so there were an enemy machine gun up there firing by six men on other side of highroad, Rfn. Ron Kinnie & eight other several other stokes & I went up fixed bayonets, Kinnie had a Bren, got two of enemy in machine gun nest, other four retreated to foot of hill & get the front of hill of ours whilst earlier in the day the back of hill had been on a fire, about twenty minutes after we opened up on machine gun nest, we all saw enemy coming from Tia Pam when it got opposite us on road it, it opened fir with machine guns on top of hill where we were none of us were wounded. We came into highway below turn in road, behind which tank was stopped, Kinnie took over the driving of trench mortar truck which apparently had no driver & brought it back to Pam Villa with Pte Rose J. & I got a drive back in it.

Dec. 22. Kinnie, Lurichie & I took up our Bren to Pill Box at Pam Villa at 0600 observed the enemy gun mortar gun on top of Bridge hill at 0900 hrs. Sgt. Winnicot took up platoon to investigate, at 1100 we were ordered up hill opposite Bridge & in front of Pam Villa at 1700 hrs, we observed enemy about 300 coming down water Catcher towards Pam Villa we came down from hill and with about 30 & 40 other soldiers & Kinnie with the Bren we fired bayonets & charged up the hill, whooping like a tribe of N. American Indians, who turned the enemy back & drove them right to top of Bridge Hill, in that charge Cpl Penney was killed & Col. Latimer was killed in front of Pam Villa, we came down from hill about 2100 hrs. too late for supper, slept outside at South Cliff Villa until 2400 was awakened by Sgt. W A Piper & put on listening post by Pam Villa until 0300 hrs. boy yapping of dogs & enemy up in hills.
Dec. 23. Fierce machine gun fire around 3 Cliff today, many snipers close, WD & Jimmy B D,
Retreated to Stanley Village, slept outside damaged.
Dec. 24. Retreated into Stanley Fort at 2100 hrs. heavy machine gun fire all the way up.
Dec. 25. OK Prepar on Parade, N.D. sheltd all day 1008 whch Kinnie killed at 1700 hrs.

comrades proud. Throughout it all, he said he tried to live a little extra for his friends buried in the Far East. "I only have one last promise to keep," Andrew said defiantly on his last day. In a weak and barely audible voice he said, "Suzuki, Frogface, Horseface, Tojo, and you, Kamloops Kid, brace yourself. I'm on my way."

Following Andrew's return from the Second World War, he kept documented proof of his experience as a combat soldier and a POW. His black "iron box" was next to his bed for the rest of his life. It was secured with a Yale padlock, and only a few family members knew about its contents. Upon his death his family discovered hundreds of genuine wartime documents within the box. They knew about his POW journals. They'd heard his many wartime stories, but the contents of the old iron box surprised everyone. It was rich in supporting documentation, the proof of his oral accounts of the horrific events he experienced.

Treasures such as the yellowed scribbler paper he'd kept in the lining of his boot throughout his internment, pressed to the bottom of the iron box. The full page, folded into a tiny square, contained Rifleman James Andrew Flanagan's handwritten account of the eighteen-day Battle of Hong Kong. Wrapped in an army-green bandage were other items, like the crow's feather that Andrew spoke of during his first day as a POW. Ando got his freedom, but the crow didn't get his feather back. The Union Jack that he rescued from Stanley Fort after the surrender was neatly rolled in the corner of the box. Many other gems of "proof" were pulled from the old iron box, including numerous letters from 1939 to 1955, enlistment papers, medical records, discharge documents, Department of National Defence photocopies of Andrew's complete records, and countless other historically significant documents. The most striking of all was Andrew's POW diaries. Written with pencil lead, the crowded pages of these little black notebooks contained the echo of Ando's war.

The Old Iron Box
by Clara Flanagan
wife of veteran James Andrew Flanagan (E30353)

Down in the musty old iron box
I found a button of tarnished gold,
A few faded letters, a belt and a hat
And a badge all covered in mold.

My hands shook as I held each one
And memories flooded my brain,
Of a proud young man, just on his way
To war, which brought great suffering and pain.

I polished the button with care
Till it shone as bright as could be,
I folded the letters from his parents dear
And set them down carefully

The hat and the belt I dusted
And the medals I rubbed and shone,
I wrapped them all in paper
And placed them back where they belonged.

All those little forgotten souvenirs
Could tell us tales so sad,
Of all the misery he had to endure
When he was just a lad.

The cold-blooded beatings he got
And the suffering he went through,
For the things he didn't believe in
He just wouldn't do.

And when he risked his life to comfort
The sick, and those who were dying,
For they were his friends
And he tried to ease their crying.

The old iron box is a treasure
It holds memories of yesterday,
Its part of the life of a dear one
And must never be thrown away.

The family will always cherish
The mementoes of long gone by,
When their dad bravely took up the torch
And was never afraid to die.

Appendix

Tables on the following pages list the Maritime Members of
The Royal Rifles of Canada at the Battle of Hong Kong.
Extracted from the HKVCA RRC list found at
http://www.hkvca.ca/cforcedata/index.php

1,977 Canadian soldiers fought in the Battle of Hong Kong.
246 were from the Maritime Provinces;
200 were from New Brunswick, including 38 from the Jacquet River area.
PEI: 4
Nova Scotia: 42
New Brunswick: 200
Total: 246

Number	Rank	Last Name	First	Second	District	Hometown	Prov.
F40903	Rifleman	ACORN	Joseph	Amon	MD 6	Peters Road	PEI
E30238	Rifleman	ADAMS	Harry	Vernon	MD 5	Campbellton	NB
E30120	Rifleman	ADAMS	Raymond	Lee	MD 5	Campbellton	NB
E30340	Rifleman	ARCHIBALD	James	Wallace	MD 5	Fredericton	NB
E30704	Rifleman	ARSENAULT	Alfred	Joseph	MD 5	Campbellton	NB
E30420	Rifleman	ARSENAULT	Andrew	A.	MD 5	Atholville	NB
E30132	Rifleman	ARSENEAU	Andrew	Joseph D.	MD 5	Upsalquitch	NB
E30133	Rifleman	ARSENEAU	Jules	D.	MD 5	Adams Gulch	NB
E30273	Rifleman	ARSENEAULT	Sylvere	A.	MD 5	Atholville	NB
F40870	Rifleman	ATWOOD	Percy	A.	MD 6	Barrington	NS
G27036	Rifleman	BABIN	Alfred	Joseph HQ Coy	MD 7	Sydney	NS
G15013	Rifleman	BANNISTER	Kenneth	Harry	MD 7	Saint John	NB
E30417	Rifleman	BARCLAY	Robert	McMillan A.	MD 5	Durham Centre	NB
E30450	Rifleman	BARCLAY	William	John C.	MD 5	Tide Head	NB
E30513	Rifleman	BASKIN	John	Angus	MD 5	Blackland	NB
F40829	Rifleman	BENT	Howard	Norman	MD 6	Halifax	NS
E30506	Rifleman	BERTIN	Edmund		MD 5	New Mills	NB

Number	Rank	Last Name	First	Second	District	Hometown	Prov.
F40905	Rifleman	BLACQUIERE	Joseph	Medius	MD 6	Nauwigewauk	NB
E30222	Rifleman	BLANCHARD	Albenie		MD 5	Val D'Amour	NB
E199	Rifleman	BLAQUIERE	Clement	W.D.	MD 5	Atholville	NB
F41001	Rifleman	BOTTIE (Pottie)	Leo	Joseph	MD 6	West Lardoise	NS
E30220	Rifleman	BOUDREAU	John	Wendall	MD 5	Balmoral	NB
E30377	Rifleman	BOUDREAU	Robert	Andrew A.	MD 5	Glen Levit	NB
E30623	Rifleman	BOUDREAU	Vance	E.B.	MD 5	Glen Levit	NB
E30705	Rifleman	BOULEY	Narcisse	B.	MD 5	Campbellton	NB
E29887	Rifleman	BRIAND	Rannie	A.	MD 5	Douglastown	NB
G18270	Rifleman	BRINE	Frederick	Alfred D.	MD 7	Port Elgin	NB
E30577	Rifleman	BROWN	Murray	Blair A.	MD 5	Hampton	NB
F40923	Rifleman	BUCHANAN	Hercules	Ralph C.	MD 6	Lockeport	NS
E30519	Rifleman	BUJOLD	Ludovic		MD 5	Charlo	NB
G17847	Rifleman	BUTLER	Gerard	Patrick	MD 7	Saint John	NB
E30471	Rifleman	CAMPBELL	Ralph	Wesley	MD 5	Campbellton	NB
G18689	Rifleman	CARR	Ashton	Frederick	MD 7	Doaktown	NB
G27223	Rifleman	CARR	Murray	Garnet D.	MD 7	Sussex	NB

Number	Rank	Last Name	First	Second	District	Hometown	Prov.
E30628	Rifleman	CHAMBERLAIN	Robert	A.	MD 5	Campbellton	NB
G27224	Rifleman	CHAMBERS	Donald	Murray	MD 7	Elgin	NB
F43639	Rifleman	CHURCHILL	George	Ralph	MD 6	Sandford	NS
E30079	Rifleman	COLE	Bliss	Thomas A.	MD 5	Sussex	NB
E30215	Staff Sergeant	COLE	Elmer	William	MD 5	Sussex	NB
E30557	Rifleman	COLE	Lewis	Alfred	MD 5	Turtle Creek	NB
E30529	Rifleman	COLE	Lloyd	Kerr	MD 5	Campbellton	NB
E30129	Corporal	COLLINS	Alger	Randolph D.	MD 5	Albert	NB
G18268	Rifleman	COMEAU	Isaac	A.	MD 7	Maltempec	NB
E30350	Rifleman	COMEAU	Martin	Joseph	MD 5	Campbellton	NB
E29950	Rifleman	CORMIER	Frank	A.	MD 5	Amherst	NS
E30346	Rifleman	CORMIER	Norman	Joseph	MD 5	Black Point	NB
E30603	Rifleman	COTTON	Leonard	J.	MD 5	Flatlands	NB
E30526	Rifleman	COURIER (Carrier)	Joseph	Arnold D.	MD 5	Belledune	NB
E30648	Rifleman	DAIGLE	Edgar	Joseph	MD 5	Campbellton	NB

Number	Rank	Last Name	First	Second	District	Hometown	Prov.
G18485	Rifleman	DARRAH	James	Cornelius D.	MD 7	West Glassville	NB
E30515	Rifleman	DEMPSEY	Joseph	Anthony Lyle	MD 5	Jacquet River	NB
F40908	Rifleman	DOIRON	John	Leo	MD 6	Hope River	PEI
E30747	Rifleman	DORAN	Alexander		MD 5	Newcastle	NB
E30317	Rifleman	DOUCET	Edgar	A.	MD 5	West Bathurst	NB
E30356	Rifleman	DRISCOLL	Abraham		MD 5	Sunnyside	NB
E30393	Rifleman	DUGUAY	Joseph	Aubin	MD 5	St. Arthur	NB
E30530	Rifleman	DUPLASSIE	Bernard	Patrick	MD 5	Upper Hills	NB
E30574	Rifleman	ELSLIGER	Alfred	William A.	MD 5	Jacquet River	NB
E30175	Rifleman	ENGLEHART	Harold	Wilfred	MD 5	Wyers Brook	NB
E29983	Rifleman	ENGLEHART	Rupert	Charles	MD 5	Wyers Brook	NB
E30578	Rifleman	EWING	Kenneth	Alexander A.	MD 5	Hampton	NB
E30016	Rifleman	FIRLOTTE	James	Blair	MD 5	Durham Centre	NB
E30508	Rifleman	FIRLOTTE	John	Fidell	MD 5	Bathurst	NB
E30212	Rifleman	FIRLOTTE	Lawrence	Joseph A.	MD 5	Campbellton	NB
E30347	Rifleman	FIRLOTTE	Leslie	Joseph	MD 5	Campbellton	NB

Number	Rank	Last Name	First	Second	District	Hometown	Prov.
E30735	Rifleman	FIRTH	Malcolm	D.	MD 5	Dawsonville	NB
E30169	Rifleman	FLANAGAN	Clifford	Allison	MD 5	Dalhousie	NB
E30353	Rifleman	FLANAGAN	James	Andrew	MD 5	Jacquet River	NB
F35248	Rifleman	FRANCIS	Earl	Foch	MD 6	Halifax	NS
E30329	Rifleman	FRENETTE	Joseph	Charles	MD 5	Glen Levit	NB
E30335	Rifleman	GALLANT	Benjamin	John (Joseph?) B.	MD 5	Glencoe	NB
E30398	Rifleman	GALLANT	Joseph	Francis	MD 5	Glencoe	NB
E30341	Rifleman	GALLIE	Phillip	James MacMillan B.	MD 5	Blackland	NB
E30522	Rifleman	GALLON	John	Wesley D.	MD 5	Black Point	NB
F40937	Rifleman	GATES	Kenneth	Harlon D.	MD 6	Kentville	NS
G32406	Corporal	GEE	John	Moffet	MD 7	Birch Ridge	NB
E30620	Rifleman	GIGNAC	Louis		MD 5	Campbellton	NB
E30289	Rifleman	GILLIS	Archie	Peter	MD 5	Judique North	NS
E30481	Rifleman	GLENDENNING	Harry	Eldon	MD 5	South Bathurst	NB
E30071	Rifleman	GRAVES	Arnold		MD 5	Anagance	NB

Number	Rank	Last Name	First	Second	District	Hometown	Prov.
E30503	Rifleman	GUITARD	Gabriel		MD 5	Nash Creek	NB
E38184	Rifleman	HACHEY	Dean	William C.	MD 5	Atholville	NB
E30416	Rifleman	HACHEY	Gerald		MD 5	West Bathurst	NB
E30113	Rifleman	HAMILTON	Sterling	Waldo	MD 5	Campbellton	NB
E30527	Rifleman	HAMILTON	Wordsworth	Wilmet D.	MD 5		NB
E30472	Rifleman	HARRIS	James	Mistie	MD 5	Campbellton	NB
E30475	Rifleman	HENRY	Thomas	Raymond	MD 5	Campbellton	NB
E30517	Rifleman	HICKEY	Charles	Gordon C.	MD 5	Nash Creek	NB
E30514	Rifleman	HICKEY	Paul	Joseph Henry	MD 5	Nash Creek	NB
E30331	Rifleman	HICKIE	William	Joseph	MD 5	Nash Creek	NB
E30570	Rifleman	HUTCHINSON	Gordon	Thomas	MD 5	Norton	NB
E30002	Rifleman	IRVINE	Bertram		MD 5	Flatlands	NB
E30172	Rifleman	IRVINE	Glenford		MD 5	Flatlands	NB
E30148	Rifleman	IRVINE	Harold	John	MD 5	Campbellton	NB
E30326	Rifleman	IRVING	Wesley	'	MD 5	Flatlands	NB
F42667	Rifleman	JACQUARD	Angus	John D.	MD 6	Little River Harbour	NS

Number	Rank	Last Name	First	Second	District	Hometown	Prov.
F40912	Rifleman	JACQUARD	Gilbert	George D.	MD 6	Comeaus Hill	NS
E30197	Corporal	JESSOP	Albert	Fred D.	MD 5	Edmundston	NB
E30584	Rifleman	JESSOP	James	Robert D.	MD 5	Edmundston	NB
F35214	Rifleman	JEWERS	Alton	Edward	MD 6	Halifax	NS
G18276	Corporal	JOHNSON	John	Seward	MD 7	Sackville	NB
E30632	Rifleman	JOHNSON	Leo		MD 5	West Bathurst	NB
E30211	Rifleman	KAINE	John	D.	MD 5	Mann Settlement	NB
E30520	Rifleman	KELLY	Frederick	Joseph	MD 5	Campbellton	NB
F40849	Rifleman	KERR	Stephen	Maxwell	MD 6	Port Williams	NS
G17892	WO Class II	KERRIGAN	Clifford	Hatfield	MD 7	Aroostook	NB
E30507	Rifleman	KILLORAN	John	Michael	MD 5	Belledune River	NB
E30548	Rifleman	KINNIE	Ronald	Murray	MD 5	Beaver Brook	NB
F93451	Staff Sergeant	LAING	John	Leslie	MD 6	Sherbrooke	NS
F40964	Rifleman	LAKE	George	Maurice A.	MD 6	Windsor	NB
E30546	Rifleman	LANDRY	Joseph	Edgar	MD 5	Charlo	NB

Number	Rank	Last Name	First	Second	District	Hometown	Prov.
E30338	Rifleman	LAPOINTE	Eugene		MD 5	Nash Creek	NB
E30362	Rifleman	LAVOIE	John	S.	MD 5	Campbellton	NB
E30006	Rifleman	LAW	Reginald		MD 5	Flatlands	NB
E30257	Rifleman	LAWRENCE	Bert	D.	MD 5	Campbellton	NB
E30494	Rifleman	LAWRENCE	Joseph	William Everett A.	MD 5	Barachois	
E30106	Rifleman	LEBEL	Valmont	A.	MD 5	Campbellton	NB
F40741	Rifleman	LEBLANC	Joseph	Napoleon	MD 6	Cape Breton	NS
E30617	Rifleman	LEBLANC	Leandre		MD 5	Campbellton	NB
E30725	Rifleman	LEBLANC	Leopold	Paul	MD 5	Campbellton	NB
E30173	Rifleman	LEBOUEF	Valmont	A.	MD 5	Campbellton	NB
E30621	Rifleman	LECOUFFE	Lionel	Joseph	MD 5	Campbellton	NB
E30399	Rifleman	LEGACY	John	Fidele D.	MD 5	Jacquet River	NB
E30228	Rifleman	LEVESQUE	Ernest	Louis	MD 5	Campbellton	NB
F77009	Rifleman	LLOYD	Ferdinand	Dallen D.	MD 6	Doctors Cove	NS
G18701	Rifleman	LOCKHART	Leighton	Orn	MD 7	Woodstock	NB
F40800	Rifleman	LOCKHART	Maurice	E.	MD 6	Greenwich	NS

Number	Rank	Last Name	First	Second	District	Hometown	Prov.
G22207 Rifleman	Rifleman	LONG	John	Richard	MD 7	Tide Head	NB
E30369	Rifleman	MCALLISTER	Arthur	D.	MD 5	Nash Creek	NB
E29964	Rifleman	MACDONALD	Alexander	John	MD 5	Wyers Brook	NB
E29974	Rifleman	MACDONALD	Allison	Ronald	MD 5	Wyers Brook	NB
E29973	Rifleman	MACDONALD	Donald		MD 5	Wyers Brook	NB
E30565	Rifleman	MACDONALD	Edward	Leonard A.	MD 5	Fredericton	NB
E29972	Rifleman	MACDONALD	George		MD 5	Wyers Brook	NB
E30370	Corporal	MACISAAC	John	Jamieson D.	MD 5	Judique North	NS
F50446	Rifleman	MACKAY	Laurie	Vincent D.	MD 6	Truro	NS
E30458	Rifleman	MACKNIGHT	Harold	Wilbur D.	MD 5	Campbellton	NB
F40988	Rifleman	MACLAUGHLIN	Thomas		MD 6	Bass River	NS
E30288	Rifleman	MACLEAN	Charles	Lewis D.	MD 5	Cape Breton	NS
E30112	Sergeant	MACMILLAN	James	Clifford Mitchell	MD 5	Campbellton	NB
F40747	Lance-Corporal	MACPHERSON	John	Francis	MD 6	Wolfville	NS
E30146	Rifleman	MAHONEY	Charles	Anthony D.	MD 5	Flatlands	NB

Number	Last Name	Rank	First	Second	District	Hometown	Prov.
E30585	MAHONEY	Rifleman	Murray	Timothy	MD 5	Sussex	NB
E30234	MAIN	Rifleman	James	Stewart D.	MD 5	Dawsonville	NB
E30179	MALLEY	Rifleman	Joseph	Maurice	MD 5	Glencoe	NB
E30022	MANN	Rifleman	Maxwell	Arthur	MD 5	Upsalquitch	NB
E29995	MANN	Rifleman	Richard	D.	MD 5	Flatlands	NB
F29629	MARSHALL	Sergeant	Albert	William D.	MD 6	Halifax	NS
E30237	MARTIN	Rifleman	Douglas	John D.	MD 5	Campbellton	NB
E30167	MARTIN	Rifleman	Paul		MD 5	Restigouche	NB
E30232	MATCHETT	Lance-Corporal	Eugene	Boyd	MD 5	Sunny Corner	NB
E30555	MAZEROLLE	Rifleman	Emile		MD 5	Peters Mills	NB
G17885	MCBEATH	Rifleman	Earl	Eldridge D.	MD 7	Ripples	NB
E29838	MCCARRON	Lance-Sergeant	Joseph	Maurice	MD 5	Harvey	NB
E30385	MCCARRON	Rifleman	Thomas	Patrick	MD 5	Benjamin River	NB
F54969	MCEACHERN	Rifleman	John	Aloysious	MD 6	Sydney	NS
G18052	MCFAWN	Rifleman	Lewis	Robert A.	MD 7	Fredericton	NB
E30562	MCGINN	Rifleman	Robert	Eugene	MD 5	Fredericton	NB

Number	Rank	Last Name	First	Second	District	Hometown	Prov.
E30702	Rifleman	MCGRATH	Jean		MD 5	Richardville	NB
E30283	Rifleman	MCGRATH	William	Joseph B.	MD 5	McGraths Cove	NB
E30528	Rifleman	MCINTYRE	George	Joseph D.	MD 5	Charlo	NB
E30672	Rifleman	MCISAAC	Joseph	Jamieson D.	MD 5	Inverness	NS
E30629	Rifleman	MCKAY	John		MD 5	Nash Creek	NB
E30625	Rifleman	MCLAUGHLIN	Robert	Arthur	MD 5	Campbellton	NB
E30375	Rifleman	MEADE	Ernest	Joseph D.	MD 5	Jacquet River	NB
E30373	Rifleman	MILLER	Ernest	James D.	MD 5	Jacquet River	NB
F140761	Rifleman	MOORE	Walter	Leslie A.	MD 6	Kentville	NS
F40841	Rifleman	MOSSMAN	Earl	Gilbert	MD 6	Saint John	NB
C48469	Rifleman	MULHERIN	Lawrence	Percival	MD 3	Grand Falls	NB
E30624	Rifleman	MURCHIE	Albert	Borden	MD 5	River Charlo	NB
E30606	Rifleman	MURPHY	Claud	Patrick	MD 5	Halifax	NS
E29975	Rifleman	MURRAY	Gordon	England D.	MD 5	Flatlands	NB
F35180	Rifleman	MYERS	Gerald	Guy A.	MD 6	Ostrea Lake	NS
E30239	Rifleman	NELLIS	Leo	Francis D.	MD 5	Flatlands	NB
F93468	Corporal	NICHOLSON	Harold	Frank	MD 6	Montague	PEI
E30504	Rifleman	NOEL	William	Henry B.	MD 5	Durham Centre	NB

Number	Rank	Last Name	First	Second	District	Hometown	Prov.
E30436	Corporal	NOLAN	Alex	Richard	MD 5	Loggieville	NB
F40192	Lance-Corporal	PALMER	George	Thomas	MD 6	St. Peters Bay	PEI
E30580	Rifleman	PATTERSON	James	Richard A.	MD 5	Sussex	NB
F34683	Rifleman	PATTINGALE	James	Reuben A.	MD 6	Maplewood	NS
G17301	Rifleman	PELLETIER	Algee	Alfred	MD 7	Edmundston	NB
E30560	Rifleman	PETE	Leo		MD 5	Culligans Belledune	NB
E30366	Rifleman	POIRIER	Levis	Joseph	MD 5	Eel River Crossing	NB
E30460	Rifleman	POLLOCK	Allison	Robert	MD 5	Glen Levit	NB
E30332	Corporal	POLLOCK	Charles	James William	MD 5	Glen Levit	NB
E30342	Rifleman	POLLOCK	Coleman		MD 5	Dawsonville	NB
E30224	Rifleman	POLLOCK	Duncan	Malcolm	MD 5	Glen Levit	NB
E30558	Rifleman	POLLOCK	Frederick	William	MD 5	Norton	NB
E30467	Rifleman	POLLOCK	Kirk	Allan	MD 5	Glen Levit	NB
E30330	Rifleman	POLLOCK	Simon	Fraser	MD 5	Campbellton	NB

Number	Rank	Last Name	First	Second	District	Hometown	Prov.
E30225	Rifleman	PORTER	Arnold	James	MD 5	Campbellton	NB
G18468	Rifleman	POST	John	Russell A.	MD 7	Aroostook	NB
E30720	Rifleman	POWERS	Vincent	Stanley	MD 5	Campbellton	NB
F29946	Rifleman	RAY	Irvin	Kirwin A.	MD 6	St. Marys River	NS
E30185	Sergeant	RICHARDS	Thomas	Medley A.	MD 5	Saint John	NB
G18211	Rifleman	RIDEOUT	William	John A.	MD 7	Bath	NB
B41548	Rifleman	RILEY	James	Clayton A.	MD 2		NB
E30123	Corporal	ROBERTS	Austin	James	MD 5	Glen Levit	NB
F40323	Rifleman	ROBLEE	Lloyd	Logan	MD 6	Springhill	NS
E30316	Rifleman	ROUSSEL	John	R.A.	MD 5	Bathurst	NB
A3625	Rifleman	ROWLAND	Roney		MD 1	Durham	NS
E38179	Rifleman	ROY	Albert	Raymond A.	MD 5	Campbellton	NB
E30452	Rifleman	ROY	Bertram	Andrew	MD 5	Jacquet River	NB
F40198	Rifleman	RUSSELL	John	David D.	MD 6	Springhill	NS
E30324	Lance-Corporal	SANNES	Aksel	George Andersen	MD 5	Campbellton	NB
F40751	Rifleman	SARTY	Perry	D.	MD 6	Mersey Point	NS
F40262	Corporal	SAVAGE	Carlyle	Fitch	MD 6	Berwick	NS

Number	Rank	Last Name	First	Second	District	Hometown	Prov.
G32318	Rifleman	SAVOY	Edward	Joseph D.	MD 7	Saint John	NB
G15004	Staff Sergeant	SCOTT	Harold	Charles	MD 7	Saint John	NB
F40361	Rifleman	SERROUL	Vincent	Russel	MD 6	Little Bras D'Or	NS
E30441	Rifleman	SHALALA	John	Alexander	MD 5	Campbellton	NB
G18280	Rifleman	SIDDALL	Hilton	Albert	MD 7	Sackville	NB
F30682	Rifleman	SIMMONS	Gordon		MD 6	South Bathurst	NB
E30186	Rifleman	SIROIS	Guy		MD 5	Albertine	NB
F40510	Corporal	SMITH	Elmer	Clifford	MD 6	Scotsburn	NB
G27295	Rifleman	SMITH	Robert	Archibald	MD 7	Glen Levit	NB
E30376	Rifleman	SMITH	Wilfred	Duncan D.	MD 5	Glen Levit	NB
E30435	Rifleman	SMITH	William	John B.	MD 5	Chatham	NB
E30461	Rifleman	SNEAR	Thomas	W.	MD 5	Campbellton	NB
E30339	Rifleman	SPLUDE	George	Raymond	MD 5	Jacquet River	NB
E30619	Rifleman	STEEVES	George		MD 5	Nash Creek	NB
F40743	Rifleman	SURETTE	Henry	Andrew D.	MD 6	Port Bickerton	NS
M61729	Rifleman	SWANSON	Kurt	S.W.	MD 13		NS

Number	Rank	Last Name	First	Second	District	Hometown	Prov.
E30622	Rifleman	SWEET	Royce	Charles	MD 5	Campbellton	NB
E30541	Rifleman	THOMPSON	Bernard	M.A.	MD 5	Glen Levit	NB
G22778	Rifleman	THOMPSON	John	Alexander	MD 7	Dawsonville	NB
E30427	Rifleman	THOMPSON	Morton	George Clinton	MD 5	Glen Levit	
E30226	Rifleman	THOMPSON	Raymond	Michael	MD 5	Campbellton	NB
G18342	Rifleman	THOMPSON	Thomas	Edward	MD 7	Richibucto	NB
E30348	Rifleman	THOMPSON	Wendell	Godfrey	MD 5	Nash Creek	NB
E30496	Rifleman	TYLER	Stanley	B.	MD 5	Campbellton	NB
E30451	Corporal	VERMETTE	Patrick		MD 5	Campbellton	NB
E30462	Rifleman	VINCENT	Kenneth	Stanley	MD 5	Campbellton	NB
E30518	Rifleman	VINCENT	Robert	Leslie	MD 5	River Charlo	NB
F29945	Rifleman	WALLACE	James	Austin B.	MD 6	Kentville	NS
G18634	Rifleman	WALSH	James	Edward	MD 7	Moncton	NB
E30582	Rifleman	WALSH	Joseph	Edward	MD 5	Penobsquis	NB
E30556	Rifleman	WATTERS	Ira	Gordon	MD 5	Apohaqui	NB
E30576	Rifleman	WEBB	James	Christopher	MD 5	Norton	NB
E30579	Rifleman	WEBB	John	Frederick	MD 5	Norton	NB

Number	Rank	Last Name	First	Second	District	Hometown	Prov.
E30489	Rifleman	WLBUR	Angus	Frank C.	MD 5	South Bathurst	NB
E30485	Rifleman	WILBUR	Clarence	Joseph G.	MD 5	South Bathurst	NB
E30374	Rifleman	WILLETT	Isaac	Alan	MD 5	Campbellton	NB
E30231	Sergeant	WILSON	Thomas	Woodrow	MD 5	Blackland	NB
E29947	Rifleman	WOODMAN	Bertram	C.A.	MD 5	Campbellton	NB
E30138	Rifleman	WYRWAS	Frederick	Arnold	MD 5	Inverness	NS

Acknowledgements

- The Royal Rifles of Canada and the Hong Kong Veterans Association.

- Hong Kong Veterans Commemorative Association.

- Lance-Corporal Phil Doddridge and Rifleman Paul Dallain, Royal Rifles of Canada veterans who fought the Battle of Hong Kong and were POWs. Both men reviewed this manuscript to ensure historical and site accuracy. Some of their terrific stories and experiences are paraphrased in this book.

- Henry Kinnie, for granting permission to quote portions of his late brother Ron Kinnie's diaries. Ron was also a Royal Rifles of Canada soldier during the Battle of Hong Kong.

- Clara Flanagan, wife of Rifleman the late James Andrew Flanagan, for granting access to all her husband's diaries, correspondence, videos, and documents.

- Gerard (Gerry) Beirne, former writer-in-residence at the University of New Brunswick and author.

- Franco David Macri, author of *Clash of Empires in South China*.

- Pre-editing volunteers Anne Marie Devereaux and Anika Duivenvoorden.

- Brent Wilson, Dr. Marc Milner, and the entire staff at the Gregg Centre for the Study of War and Society at UNB.

- The series co-publisher, Goose Lane Editions, particularly Julie Scriver and Martin Ainsley, and copy editor Jess Shulman.

- All volunteer readers who confirmed the potential of *The Endless Battle*.

- A special thanks to Alfred's brother Donald Elsliger for allowing his poem to be published in this manuscript.

- Steve Flanagan, Photography and Image Enhancement

Selected Bibliography

Manuscript Sources

J. Andrew Flanagan Collection of military and veteran affairs records and personal correspondence.

Diary of Rifleman J. Andrew Flanagan. The Battle of Hong Kong December, December 6-25, 1941.

Diary of Rifleman J. Andrew Flanagan. Prisoner of War, December 1941 to October 1945.

Diary of Rifleman Ron Kinnie, Royal Rifles of Canada, October to December 1941.

Diary of Sergeant Lance Ross, Royal Rifles of Canada.

Diary of Corporal Edmund William Shayle, Winnipeg Grenadiers.

Diary of Private Charles Richards Trick, Winnipeg Grenadiers.

Secondary Sources

Banham, Tony. *Sinking of the Lisbon Maru: Britain's Forgotten Wartime Tragedy*. Hong Kong: Hong Kong University Press, 2010.

Bell, Christopher M. "'Our Most Exposed Outpost': Hong Kong and British Far Eastern Strategy, 1921-1941." *Journal of Military History* 60, no. 1 (1996).

Copp, Terry. "The Defence of Hong Kong: December 1941." *Canadian Military History* 10, no. 4 (2001).

Endacott, G.B. *Hong Kong Eclipse*. New York: Oxford University Press, 1978.

Fedorowich, Kent. "Cocked Hats and Swords and Small, Little Garrisons: Britain, Canada and the Fall of Hong Kong, 1941." *Modern Asian Studies* 37, no. 1 (2003).

Garneau, Grant. *The Royal Rifles of Canada in Hong Kong, 1941-1945.* Hong Kong Veterans Association, Quebec-Maritimes Branch. Sherbrooke, PQ: Progressive Publications, 1980.

Greenhous, Brereton. *"C" Force to Hong Kong: a Canadian Catastrophe, 1941-1945.* Toronto: Dundurn Press, 1997.

Lindsay, Oliver. *The Battle for Hong Kong 1941-1945: Hostage to Fortune.* Hong Kong: Hong Kong University Press, 2005.

MacDonell, George S. *One Soldier's Story.* Toronto: Dundurn Press, 2002.

Macri, Franco David. *Clash of Empires in South China: The Allied Nations' Proxy War with Japan, 1935-1941.* Lawrence, KS: University Press of Kansas, 2012.

Macri, Franco David. "C Force to Hong Kong: The Price of Collective Security in China, 1941." *Journal of Military History* 77 (January 2013): 141-71.

Man, Kwong Chi, and Tsoi Yiu Lun. *Eastern Fortress: A Military History of Hong Kong, 1840-1970.* Hong Kong: Hong Kong University Press, 2014.

Vance, Jonathan F. *Bamboo Cage: The P.O.W. Diary of Flight Lieutenant Robert Wyse, 1942-1943.* Fredericton: Goose Lane Editions and The New Brunswick Military Heritage Project, 2009.

Veterans Affairs Canada. *Canadians in Hong Kong.* Ottawa, 2005.

Online Resources

Doddridge, Lance-Corporal Phil. *Edgar's Story of the Bicycle.* http://www.hkvca.ca/memoriesuninvited/Chapter%203.htm.

Hong Kong Veterans Commemorative Association website. http://www.hkvca.ca/index.htm.

National Film Board of Canada, *The Valour and Horror* series. Episode 1: "Savage Christmas." Directed by Brian McKenna. www.nb.cafilm/savagechristmashongkong1941.

Index

The New Brunswick Military History Museum

The mission of the New Brunswick Military History Museum is to collect, preserve, research, and exhibit artifacts which illustrate the history and heritage of the military forces in New Brunswick and New Brunswickers at war, during peacetime, and on United Nations or North Atlantic Treaty Organization duty.

The New Brunswick Military History Museum is proud to partner with the Gregg Centre.

Highlighting 400 years of New Brunswick's history.

The New Brunswick Military Heritage Project

The New Brunswick Military Heritage Project, a non-profit organization devoted to public awareness of the remarkable military heritage of the province, is an initiative of the Brigadier Milton F. Gregg, VC, Centre for the Study of War and Society of the University of New Brunswick. The organization consists of museum professionals, teachers, university professors, graduate students, active and retired members of the Canadian Forces, and other historians. We welcome public involvement. People who have ideas for books or information for our database can contact us through our website: www.unb.ca/nbmhp.

One of the main activities of the New Brunswick Military Heritage Project is the publication of the New Brunswick Military Heritage Series with Goose Lane Editions. This series of books is under the direction of J. Brent Wilson, Director of the New Brunswick Military Heritage Project at the University of New Brunswick. Publication of the series is supported by grants from the Province of New Brunswick and the Canadian War Museum.

The New Brunswick Military History Series

Volume 1
Saint John Fortifications, 1630-1956,
Roger Sarty and Doug Knight

Volume 2
Hope Restored: The American Revolution and the Founding of New Brunswick, Robert L. Dallison

Volume 3
The Siege of Fort Beauséjour, 1755, Chris M. Hand

Volume 4
Riding into War: The Memoir of a Horse Transport Driver, 1916-1919, James Robert Johnston

Volume 5
The Road to Canada: The Grand Communications Route from Saint John to Quebec, W.E. (Gary) Campbell

Volume 6
Trimming Yankee Sails: Pirates and Privateers of New Brunswick, Faye Kert

Volume 7
War on the Home Front: The Farm Diaries of Daniel MacMillan, 1914-1927,
edited by Bill Parenteau and Stephen Dutcher

About the Author

Andy Flanagan was born in the small rural New Brunswick community of Belledune, the third child in a family of eight. *The Endless Battle* is based on his father's war experiences. Andy's writing has appeared in the *Northern Light*, the *Ottawa Citizen*, and on CBC.ca. He is a member and past director of the Writers' Federation of New Brunswick, a regional executive member of the Hong Kong Veterans Commemorative Association, a member of the Royal Canadian Legion, and an active participant in a regional environmental group.